Proof of Reiki, Proof of Eternity

Torsten A. Lange

By the same author:

Reiki (Hay House, 2017), reissued as *Reiki Made Easy* (2018)

TORSTEN A. LANGE

Proof of Reiki, Proof of Eternity

Discover the *hidden* dimension of Reiki -
and find answers to life's biggest questions

ReikiScience Publications

London I Los Angeles

To Mum

My amazing companion
through eternity

Contents

Part III: The Universe

Prologue

On 13th February 2016, just after 6 p.m., I had the strangest experience of my life. I saw a mirage.

Only it wasn't in the desert, and I could have a conversation with it. Or rather, *him*.

I was on my second research trip to Japan, *en route* to a little village called Taniai, the birthplace of Mikao Usui, the founder of Reiki. As it was a few hours' drive, my guide and interpreter, Michi, had kindly volunteered to take me there and booked us into a hotel on the way.

So far, I had only stayed in Western-style hotels, and this one was billed as traditional Japanese, so naturally I was a bit nervous. But the staff were truly welcoming, I ended up with a bed rather than the mat I had expected, and Michi even managed to organise a vegetarian dinner for me. So far, so good.

Over the road there was an *onsen* – a public bath fed by natural hot springs. As hotel guests, we had free entry, and Michi suggested we go there before dinner. We changed into *yukata* from the hotel – I looked absolutely hilarious in this cross between a dressing gown and a kimono – and quickly ran over the road. Icy rain was falling, the temperature was near freezing, and we were wearing flip-flops.

All *onsen* are divided into male and female sections. Some have only one pool on each side, but this place had an entire range –

1

some inside the building, others in the beautifully designed grounds. It was a proper spa resort.

As it was nearly closing time, most visitors were leaving, and I suppose no more than ten were left in the men's section. I went outside and tried a few pools that were covered by wooden roofs, but was drawn to one that was completely open. It was so shallow that I had to lie down to submerge myself in the hot water, though the rain was still hitting my face.

The grounds were gently lit and the beauty and tranquillity almost surreal. After a while, though, the rain on my face started to get a bit much and I turned over to lie on my front.

That was when it happened.

Slowly, I lifted my head ... and noticed I wasn't alone anymore. Outside the pool, about 15 feet away, was one of the big decorative stones you often find in meditation gardens in Japan. And a man was sitting on it and looking at me. Only he wasn't a 'real' man, made of flesh and blood, but more like a 3-D image. A mirage. A projection.

'This is a figment of my imagination!' I told myself.

I looked away and the man disappeared.

'Good. My mind isn't really playing tricks then.'

I recovered for a moment, then slowly turned back again ... and to my surprise, the man was there again. Sitting on the stone, smiling.

And the face was unmistakable: it was Mikao Usui, the founder of Reiki.

I looked around the *onsen* to see whether there was anybody who could witness this strange encounter, but I was the only one there. Michi was at the other end of the grounds in a hot tub. I could just make out the back of his head. Everybody else was indoors.

Then Usui started talking to me.

I can't say that my position, lying on my front and straining my neck to see the man outside the bath, was particularly comfortable, but I was too mesmerised to move.

The conversation must have lasted about 20 minutes and often went into remarkable detail. I'll go into it all later. But for now, let me just tell you how it ended.

Mikao Usui said, very matter-of-factly, 'You will bring Reiki into the 21st century.'

Then he disappeared.

I was left completely puzzled. What now? *How* was I supposed to bring Reiki into the 21st century? Wasn't it already there? I was a Reiki teacher, yes, but it seemed such a strange task, I had no idea how to begin. I was also rather hesitant about sharing this strange encounter, especially after a friend kindly suggested it would completely ruin my reputation.

In the end, bringing Reiki into the 21st century turned out to be a puzzle with each piece appearing one by one, over a number of years. The final piece was the first scientific proof of the different vibrational levels of Reiki – indeed, of the universe.

The closer the puzzle got to completion, the more I realised that the framework had been laid a long time before. So, to reveal the complete picture, I have to go back to the beginning...

Part I

London

1.

Rock Bottom

I will never forget the day Mum and I decided to commit suicide.

We were sitting in the cluttered living room cum live-in office where we had planned to get our lives back together. It hadn't worked.

I was the first to bring it up. 'I can't go on anymore. I want to get out. What … if we just ended our lives?'

As strange as it may sound, Mum and I were so close that I didn't even consider doing it on my own.

She nodded. She felt the same.

'What if we jumped off a bridge? That would do it. No more worries.'

Mum nodded again.

Then we just sat in silence.

I was puzzled. How the hell did we get here? Where did we go wrong? How did we *deserve* this?

For the first 30 years of my life, everything had gone so well: I had been pretty good at school and become the youngest head prefect in its history; I had received a medal of honour during my time doing National Service; I had got a master's degree in political science and become chairman of the local branch of the Christian Democratic Party (again the youngest in its history); I had started my own business selling silverware and antiques, and after a few years I had been running a small chain of stores and holding regular retail exhibitions in every major German city.

When I turned 30, I decided to expand internationally, moved to the UK, opened a store on London's famous Regent Street, started a wholesale business to the USA and began designing my own jewellery ranges. Needless to say, I felt pretty pleased with myself.

Then suddenly things started to go wrong. Foot-and-mouth disease swept through the British countryside, and rather than vaccinating the animals, the government reacted with mass killings to prevent it from spreading further. There were two kinds of casualties: over 6 million cows and sheep – and me.

Standing in my store on Regent Street, I just didn't understand where my customers had gone. With images of burning piles of corpses dominating global news for weeks, many tourists were hesitant about coming to Britain. Americans stayed away almost completely, and they had made up 80 per cent of my customers. So turnover was 80 per cent down, while the astronomical overheads stayed the same.

I tried anything and everything to stem the tide, but it was too late. My business went bankrupt. And, given that I had personally guaranteed the loans, I followed suit. My trendy apartment in Notting Hill was lost, along with my flat in Berlin, and even the family home in Hamburg. Unsurprisingly, my relationship didn't survive the turmoil either.

In the end, Mum and I couldn't even afford the rent for the small house we had moved to. We were homeless.

And this, of course, was the worst of it: I was responsible for Mum.

I felt terrible about getting her into this situation. She had always been there for me. At school, she had supported me in my often precocious endeavours; in politics, she had canvassed for me during election campaigns; we had set up the business in Germany together; and a year after I had moved to London and she and Dad had divorced, she joined me there, basing herself just round the corner from where I lived. When I was away, she ran the business, and she was responsible for many of the designs in our store. Often, one of us would start a piece and the other would finish it. We had similar tastes in art, music, even food. She had turned 60 just after the bankruptcy and had devoted much of her life to me. And I had brought her to this...

Some lovely friends offered us their spare bedrooms, so we were never actually without a roof over our heads, but living with others is very different from having your own place. A few weeks later, other friends asked us to stay with them in the countryside, so we moved there, only to be politely asked whether we would mind leaving again a fortnight later, as their daughter wanted to come up for the weekend. So the first friends took us in again. Our belongings were in the boot of my car. Luckily, the insolvency service had left me with it – it wasn't worth trying to cash in a 12-year-old vehicle.

Somehow we kept going. If one of us felt down, the other tried to cheer them up. Or we would simply cry together.

After a few months, through selling our collection of antique furniture, and with some additional help from friends and family, we managed to rent a small place. We couldn't believe our luck! Operation Recovery started straight away: with the materials we had left, we created new jewellery collections, got a contract to design for a French fashion house and had a new idea every week.

Not a single one worked out.

And no matter what job I applied for, I didn't get it. Mind you, given that I had been self-employed all my life, I probably wouldn't have employed myself either.

A year later, we hit rock bottom again. In economic terms, I think this is called a double-dip recession. We were so far behind with our rent, our landlord was threatening to evict us. And this time, we had run out of hope. Hadn't we already tried everything?

All this was going through my mind while Mum and I sat there in silence. I still didn't know why this had happened to us, but one thing was obvious: suicide was the only way out.

Today, many of my students come on my courses because I have freely shared these experiences. They are also going through tough times. Often unbearable times. And it is reassuring to know that there are others who know how hard life can be.

Of course, they also come to learn something – a healing modality called Reiki. They come in the hope that it might do for them what it did for Mum and me: bring positive change.

The very day Reiki came into our lives, things changed for the better. Tangibly, physically, materially und ultimately spiritually. It was so unbelievable that we initially didn't even realise that it was Reiki that had been the turning-point. But the evidence was unmistakable.

The following ten years became a journey of finding out how this was possible. How could 'energy healing' have an impact on life circumstances?

I slowly began to understand quantum physics, and its basic assumption that all energy is connected. If one thing changes, our entire energy field reacts. And if the change is brought about by particularly high vibrations, like light, then everything can brighten up.

A few years ago, I finally found myself saying, 'Thank you, universe, for my bankruptcy!' But it took a while to get there…

2.

Saved, for Now

Mum was the first to break the silence. 'I completely understand. I feel exactly the same. I don't see any point in carrying on either.'

There was another long pause.

Then she added, 'But we can't do it. It isn't just about us. We'll affect other people as well. Most of them will get over it, but your sister won't. There's no way she'll be able to live with the guilt. And we can't ruin other people's lives too.'

My sister, eight years younger than me, had just finished studying. Still living in Germany, she had helped out when she could, but of course her resources were limited. I thought about her. If we killed ourselves, how would she cope? Was there any way she could? Probably not.

As so often, Mum was right. We couldn't just sneak out at somebody else's expense. But how could we possibly carry on living?

I was angry. Angry with myself, angry with the universe, angry that we couldn't even kill ourselves.

Why had this happened? *Why* had it happened *to us*? Why? Why? Why?

I didn't have a clue. And yet, another thought came into my mind. Even though I didn't understand it, there *might* be a reason for it all.

This was prompted by a strange experience. Two years before, just a few weeks after the collapse of my business, my friend Susan had phoned and asked if I had any plans for the following Wednesday. Of course I didn't. With no business to run, I was just sitting at home feeling depressed. So she said, 'I'll take you to the Spiritualist Association of Great Britain for a reading with a medium – it'll be a little present!'

I'd never heard of mediums before. *Media*, yes, but TV and newspapers were obviously something different. A few enquiries later, I began to understand that mediums were people who conveyed messages. But *understand* is probably not the right word. Because the messages came from the dead.

I didn't have a clue how this worked. When you're dead, you're dead. Aren't you?

I wasn't a complete stranger to paranormal messages – I'd seen a clairvoyant before, I'd had a Tarot card reading, and a lady in Hong Kong had read my palm. Some information had been helpful, some rather imprecise. And not one scrap of it had been able to prevent my misery, or even predict it. But I had nothing to lose now, so I agreed to go with Susan. At least I'd get out of the house for an afternoon.

The next week I met Susan outside a rather grand building in London's embassy quarter, a bequest to the Spiritualist Association as it turned out. The medium I was going to meet apparently came highly recommended. Susan said he was booked out weeks in advance. A little reassured to discover there were other people making use of such strange offerings, I purchased a tape at reception so that I could listen to the sitting again at home and went inside for my appointment.

In contrast to the grand façade, the tiny box-room I was led to was pretty basic. There were just two chairs and a little table with an old-fashioned tape recorder on it. One chair was occupied by a rather large man, around 60 I guessed, who smiled broadly when I entered and asked me to sit down. His name was Keith Hall and I was surprised to find him so, well, *normal*. Almost the prototype of normal. He later told me that he'd started his working life as a butcher, then gone on to own a fish-and-ship shop and a seaside hotel. An ordinary guy with an ordinary career. What followed, however, was completely out of the ordinary.

Switching on the tape recorder, Keith dived straight in.

'I see a lot of teaching around you... Were any of your ancestors teachers?'

That brought me up short. He was absolutely right: *many* of my ancestors were teachers.

He went on: 'I also see music and the theatre...'

Again, he was right. Spot on, in fact. More than half of the ancestors I am aware of on my father's side were musicians, many of them playing in theatres.

'There is one who was a pianist. He was particularly famous.'

Ah yes, my great grand uncle August Främcke was a famous pianist who played all over the world, including for royalty, and became the director of the New York College of Music at the beginning of the 20th century.

'I also hear "Austria". Have you got any family connections there?'

That man could have guessed any country in the world – and been wrong. For generations, my family has always been German – with the exception of my grandfather, who was ... *Austrian*!

I was utterly amazed, and this was just the beginning. Keith was getting more and more specific.

'There is somebody called Alfred, who is holding his chest ... I think he wants to show me that this was the cause of his death. Most of the spirits around you need an interpreter, as they speak German, so it's lucky I have an interpreter in the spirit world, but this guy doesn't. He speaks very academic English and sends his regards to your mother.'

It will probably come as no surprise to you now that I had an uncle called Alfred who died from a lung condition and was a university professor, lecturing worldwide. In *English*, of course. And he got on particularly well with Mum.

The main person who came through, though, was my grandfather.

'He tells me that you should go on a computer course.'

What a strange thing to say – I knew the basics already and had no particular inclination to learn more. And of course there were no computers around when my grandfather was alive.

'He also says there is somebody called C'sima – that's what it sounds like – around you. She is reading a book that you should read too – it will answer many of your questions.'

My sister, Cosima, was reading Neale Donald Walsch's *Conversations with God* at the time and had already given me a copy as a present. I'd categorized it as typical fantasy material that would only work for people who believed in such obscure stuff, and hadn't even opened it. Perhaps I should.

The reading with Keith lasted 30 minutes and I left in a state of shock. And awe. I'd had a *conversation with the dead*! Or rather, as that wasn't technically possible, I'd been made aware, in pretty unmistakable terms, that there was no such thing as death. *There was only life – before and after death.*

It took quite a few more years to realise that this understanding is at the very core of Reiki. But my experience with Keith showed that it's not exclusive to Reiki. Reiki is just one of the many ways of receiving support and guidance from beyond.

All these years later, I cannot express how grateful I am to Susan for taking me to this reading! And yet I can't help thinking that the idea wasn't strictly hers. Surely she must have been guided to do it. After all, she could have taken me for dinner (which, incidentally, she also did), she could have given me a good book, or she could have taken me to see a career coach. Instead, she arranged an appointment with the spirit world.

I'd been planning to ask some questions about my future: how and when life would get better. What to do next. But somehow I didn't get round to it. I suppose that wasn't the point. That reading wasn't about life, it was about death – about giving evidence that life doesn't end with death. It wasn't about my career, it was about my spiritual path.

I went home and started to read *Conversations with God*. Over the next few weeks, it expanded my awareness even further. The most amazing thing was that it actually made sense! It was the first time that I had read something spiritual that I could wholeheartedly believe. It simply felt right.

It was also the first time that I had come across the use of the word 'God' in a non-personal sense. There was no grumpy old man snorting at you; instead, there was something that could best be described as 'awareness'. And the book was the opposite of lofty. It was colloquial, cool and straight to the point. For me, it was an entirely new approach to spiritual subjects. You could say that it brought God down to Earth. The key message I took away with me was: *This life is just one of numerous incarnations. You are here to experience, to learn and grow. Make the most of this opportunity.* This message blended perfectly with the experience I'd just had. And, after all, it had been recommended by 'the other side'. What more can you ask for?

When I look back today, though, I realise that my understanding was mainly intellectual. I wasn't embodying it. And the life changes I was desperate for still didn't materialise. I may have had a connection to heaven, but my life on Earth was a mess.

There were days when Mum and I could hardly afford basic food. We never really starved, and I got remarkably creative with pasta and potato dishes, but it led to some strange situations, for example when we were going into town on one of our many unsuccessful attempts to make a business project work and got a Thai stir-fry from a market stall for lunch. We could only afford one, so we shared it, but I was too embarrassed to ask for a second fork, so we ended up sharing the cutlery too. Our struggles had obviously had an effect on our confidence as well.

Another time I was smarter and made preparations in advance: before I walked into a job interview, I took my coat off and carried it over my arm so that they wouldn't see how torn the lining was. But I still didn't get the job.

At one stage I started looking at people begging in the streets and wondered if that would be my last resort. If I went further afield, somewhere Mum wouldn't see me, it might be an option.

Around this time, a good friend saw me walking around a shopping area and didn't even recognize me at first. Leaning forward and walking slowly, I looked, he said, like an old man. I was 35 at the time.

After recognising me, he bought me a new coat.

Strangely, all this was happening at a time when the economy was generally doing well. None of our friends or wider family was suffering anything similar. Very kindly, some of them offered financial support, but it normally lasted for just a few weeks, and almost made things worse. We just couldn't bear asking for help or living on another people's mercy anymore. And most of the support was lent to us, too, so we felt compelled to give regular updates and estimates of when we would be able to repay it. Of course, we didn't have a clue.

We read more and more spiritual books, many of which made a lot of sense, but our circumstances didn't change. Were we missing something vital? Or were we wrong to hope?

It was at this point, two years after the loss of the business, when every opportunity had slipped through our fingers and nothing had materially changed, that Mum and I had the suicide conversation.

It wasn't just concern for my sister that held me back. There was another reason too. A possibility. If *Conversations with God* was right, there was a reason for everything. Everything was part of a journey, part of an experience. So, if there was indeed a lesson to learn here, even though I didn't have a clue what it was, what would happen if we didn't see it through? Would we have to come back and go through something similar again?

The more I thought about it, the more this started to make sense. And going through *all this* again, in another life, was *the last thing* I wanted to happen. Better get it over with in *this* one.

So we decided to hang around. For now.

I often ask myself whether I really wanted to commit suicide. I'm not sure we would really have gone through with it. Psychologists say that if people talk about it, they are less likely to do it. But I honestly just couldn't see how I could carry on living.

Life can be horrible. I really mean that. Looking at the news, we see horrors every day. Indeed, you may be in the depths of despair right now.

19

But please let me tell you one thing: there *is* light at the end of the tunnel.

3.

Reiki for Christmas

Years later, I had the privilege of telling Neale Donald Walsch this story in person. He was running the first of a series of retreats at Montserrat monastery in Catalunya and I was a participant. What an amazing opportunity that was! And what amazing timing, for I had the honour of being invited to run the next retreat there.

Neale Donald Walsch's retreat was about *Conversations with God*. Mine was about the power of Reiki. I called it 'Living the Light'. By that time, Reiki had truly lit up my life.

For a while after that afternoon with Mum, though, the darkness continued. Deciding to live is one thing, being able to live is quite another. And even if I could somehow muddle through myself, how could I safeguard Mum? I couldn't bear seeing her suffer any longer.

So I came up with a rather drastic idea. I had found a website, primarily a dating site, that featured a section on 'professional services'. Perhaps I could offer them. We needed to survive. I had to do something.

I remember coming home from the supermarket yet again with potatoes and tomatoes and thinking about it. Despite all my other problems, I'd never found it difficult to meet guys for a date. They'd somehow chat me up and we'd meet once or twice. I was too pre-occupied with sorting out my life to be ready for a relationship, though. And I wanted an equal relationship, not one in which I was dependent. Or maybe the right guy simply hadn't turned up yet.

But, doing it for money? Well, what did I have to lose? I sent an email to the website asking for the prerequisites and terms and conditions. There was just one: £40 per week to be listed with a photo. I didn't have the money, so I waited.

A few days later I visited a friend – quite a rare event, as I usually couldn't afford the train fare into town. This friend knew that and lovingly offered to pay it for me. On the journey, I had a look around: all these men could be my clients. Possibly well-paying clients.

But could I really do it? I realised I couldn't. Not even if they'd had a shower beforehand. I just couldn't disconnect mutual attraction from sex. It wouldn't work.

On the way back, I was even more frustrated. Another chance gone. I kept quiet about it and not even Mum knew until she saw this manuscript. But I've never forgotten that despair can lead to doing things we would never consider in normal circumstances, and I've always kept the email from the dating site as a reminder not to judge others by what they do. Who knows what despair they are facing?

Soon after that, a small change took place: we discovered that we were eligible for benefits. So far we'd survived by selling the antique furniture and jewellery we had left (including Mum's wedding band, which paid for the food for a week), and taking advantage of the occasional help from friends and family. Now we had the council paying the rent, which was a great help.

In addition, I received £50 per week unemployment benefit. It was better than nothing, but it really wasn't much to pay for food, clothing, utilities, petrol and dog food. The one thing that cheered me up was cuddling the two Yorkshire terriers that my ex-partner had left behind. But why wasn't anybody offering me a job? What the hell was I supposed to do?

Finally, a friend mentioned that one of his relatives could do with some help with her cleaning business. In the end, my wages barely paid my travel costs, but I got an idea: why not do this myself? Within a few weeks, I'd started a small business offering professional cleaning to landlords and estate agents. And my life started to get back on track. Slowly.

But a big change did come. One afternoon, collecting the keys for a place I was due to clean, I overheard the estate agents discussing the refurbishment of a flat. Did anyone know a good decorator?

'I can do it,' I said, trying to sound as confident as possible. And I got the job.

I had almost no experience, but I consulted DIY books, equipped myself with filler, sandpaper and paint, and got started. The job took three times longer than planned, but no one complained. In fact, everybody appeared pleased with the result and the flat was rented out at one of the very first viewings.

That was the start I needed. I was offered more decorating jobs, and before long I could pay our rental arrears, have my car repaired and do a normal weekly shop at the supermarket. Six months later, we moved to a bigger home, complete with a garage and a small workshop. I worked seven days a week, often until midnight. But the worries had started to subside and the forgotten feeling of freedom was beginning to return.

About a year later, as I was reflecting on these changes, suddenly something clicked. Something big. How could I not have noticed before?

Thinking back to when I started my first refurbishment job, I remembered how apologetic Mum had been about leaving me on my own that day. But there had been a good reason for it. A few months earlier, my sister had sent her a present: a German book about somebody's spiritual awakening. This guy had started to learn a complementary therapy called Reiki. Everybody could learn it, he said; everybody could get healing hands. And it could be applied to every aspect of life.

Mum decided she *had* to learn it. She somehow managed to put some money aside each week until she had the funds for a weekend course. It started on a Friday – the day I started my first decorating project.

Now the penny finally dropped: the day Reiki came into our lives, they changed for the better.

Mum came back from her course and started to place her hands on anything and everything she felt could benefit from Reiki: the dogs, the car, me.

And I felt something. As soon as she placed her hands on my back, it got remarkably warm beneath them.

'Good for her,' I thought. 'And now I'm going to move on to something important. Working hard to get us back on track, for instance.'

But Mum had other plans: I had to learn Reiki too. And, as I clearly had other priorities, she came up with a fool-proof idea: a Reiki course for Christmas.

4.

Healing Hands

Completely oblivious to the impact Reiki had already had on our lives, a few weeks later I attended my first Reiki course. It wasn't as exciting as I hoped.

First, I found the small group of students rather strange. I would have preferred to have been on my own. Although life was slowly getting better, I was still very much in what I would call a 'victim bubble'. I felt that there were few people who had suffered as I had. When the ice started to break during the tea breaks, though, I was gobsmacked when I realised that I wasn't the only one experiencing problems. In fact, we all had one thing in common: our problems had led us to try Reiki.

Looking back a decade later, having trained thousands of students, it has become obvious to me that most people don't learn Reiki out of interest, but out of necessity. Either they or the people around them are in huge distress. And, just as in my own life, the extraordinary amount of feedback I have received makes it clear that Reiki can provide a turning-point.

The real question about Reiki is not whether it helps, but how. And, possibly, why the help is needed in the first place…

Back on that first course, there was no big bang. Not even during the key element: the attunements.

Attunements are what sets Reiki apart from other healing modalities. They are rituals or techniques designed to open or deepen the connection to the Reiki energy. Without an attunement, Reiki cannot be used.

During the course, everyone had four of them. In small groups, we were led into an adjacent room, asked to sit on a chair and close our eyes and told that a bell would signal the start of the ritual. It all felt rather mysterious (today I explain much more before an attunement, so that students can experience it with more ease). We sat down and the bell rang. About 15 minutes later, it rang again, and the teacher announced that the attunement was now complete.

I still remember my disappointment. All I could think was: 'That's typical! I'm just not intuitive enough for this stuff. Not open enough. Not positive enough.' I hadn't felt anything at all. Not that I'd expected to feel much, but I'd thought there would be *something* – a subtle vibration, some kind of experience. Instead, I'd been sitting and waiting, and then it was all over before it had even started. I don't recall much exciting feedback from my fellow students either.

But there were four attunements, and during the second I did have an unexpected experience: I saw purple. I saw a colour with my eyes closed.

It took me quite a while to figure out that seeing colours with your eyes closed means that your mind is translating energetic vibrations into a visual experience. It is one of the fundamental ways in which we can see Reiki working – and provides an explanation that goes right back to the very first Reiki attunement in history.

It would take several years for me to understand this connection, but even after the very first attunement, although I had felt nothing at all, when we continued with the class and I had my hands on my thighs, as you do when you are relaxed and in listening mode, I noticed that my thighs were getting warm. Then hot. So hot that it was almost uncomfortable. When I took my hands off, the heat subsided; when I put them back, it was there again. It wasn't body heat. It wasn't sweat. I was something different, something new.

All the way home on the underground I was putting my hands on my body and taking them off – on, off, on, off, on my ears, on my eyes, on the top of my head, on my shoulders, my arms, my torso, my thighs. It must have been hilarious to watch, but I didn't care. I didn't understand why, but it was undeniable: I had what today I term 'healing hands'. I had Reiki!

And if *I* could learn it, I concluded that everybody could.

I took three things away from that Reiki course. First, I had healing hands. That was as unexpected as it was amazing. Second, I should use Reiki every day on myself – that was the most important piece of advice I ever got about its use. And third, the colour purple. Whatever that meant.

I certainly left with many more questions than answers. But I did know Reiki wasn't dependent on openness or readiness to receive it (at least not consciously), or on affirmations or positive thinking. In short, from day one I knew that Reiki wasn't a placebo. It was real.

5.

Getting Practical

My Reiki journey had started. I went back home and started using my healing hands. On myself. I love cooking, and at least twice a week I would cut myself when chopping the vegetables, grating garlic and ginger or slicing bread. Although these cuts weren't normally very deep, for some odd reason they would be constantly inflamed and often take more than a week to heal. Once I even got a series of antibiotics prescribed by my GP, but as soon as I finished it, the problem was back. With Reiki now at my disposal, whenever I cut a finger, I would simply hold it under some cold water for a moment, then place my other hand over it and give it Reiki.

To be honest, though, 'give it Reiki' isn't a very good description, as I didn't really do anything, I just used my intention to 'switch Reiki on' and let it flow. Most of the time I couldn't find the cut again the next day. It had healed within hours.

The first 'professional' treatment I gave was to a staff member at the estate agent's I was working for. They were my main source of income, so no pressure...! Constantly working overtime, this woman was stressed out. Headaches, colds – the usual results. I had just bought a treatment couch and invited her to come over the following week.

What would she expect? What would she feel? Understandably, I was nervous. After an hour, when she got up from the treatment couch, I held my breath.

Looking half-excited, half-confused, she just said, 'Wow... I didn't expect that at all. That was amazing!'

She didn't give me any specifics. But I thought it was a good start.

Many people struggle to find the words to describe a Reiki treatment. It took a while for me to accept that 'unexpected', 'different' or even 'surreal' were meant to be complimentary. But I started to offer Reiki to anybody and everybody, and have ever since.

Opportunities turned up everywhere. On holiday, I met a man suffering from a really bad cold and looking pretty miserable. I offered him Reiki and just asked him to sit on a sun-lounger on the beach while I placed my hands on his head. Twenty minutes later, his headache had gone, and he enjoyed the rest of his holiday much more.

I gave Reiki to my greyhound when she lost a toenail and was bleeding and in pain, and the bleeding stopped almost immediately.

One day I saw a poorly-looking fly crawling along my windowsill and falling over every few steps. When I got closer, I noticed that it actually had a little part of its wings clipped, probably due to an accident. I gently placed it on a little piece of paper, carried it outside and put it on a flower. But I couldn't really just leave the poor little creature on its own – it was obvious that it needed help. So I gave it Reiki for a few minutes, and when I lifted my hands again, it actually flew away. With a partially clipped wing!

Running in a park in Berlin when I was visiting my sister, I saw some adults standing around a girl who was lying on the floor crying. She had just jumped off a wall that was slightly higher than she had thought and had hurt her ankle.

The adults were her teachers and it turned out that they were on a school trip. They asked me if I knew how to call a professional first-aider and we eventually found a number and called for an ambulance. But as the poor girl was still crying, I wondered whether it would be appropriate to offer Reiki.

Fortunately, Berlin's Accident Hospital, teaching hospital for the University Hospital Charité, has a Reiki department, so I had a point of reference. I explained that it was an unintrusive therapy and I wouldn't need to physically touch the girl. I asked her if she was okay to receive Reiki, then knelt down next to her, placed my hands above her ankle and let Reiki flow. After a few minutes she stopped crying, looked at me with the most amazing expression of astonishment and said that the pain was actually getting better.

I thought I'd do a little test and moved my hands both further up her leg and down towards her toes. As soon as they were above her ankles, I could feel the difference – a tingling in my palms – so it was clear where the problem was. However, the difference wasn't as strong as I had expected. I was therefore pretty sure that the injury wasn't as serious as the teachers had first thought and the ankle wasn't actually broken.

When the paramedics eventually came, they asked the girl to move her foot from side to side and roll it around. Then they said,

'It looks very much like a sprain. As we're already here, we'll take her to hospital just to make sure that everything is okay. But based on the tests so far, it doesn't look like a fracture.'

Reiki practitioners aren't supposed to diagnose, but it's interesting to see where intuition can lead.

Sometimes there was even a direct contrast between Reiki and non-Reiki. A friend of mine asked me if I could give her some Reiki after tooth surgery, and of course I did. A few weeks later, more surgery was due, but she didn't want to bother me again, as she assumed I was busy. The third time, however, she asked for Reiki again and told me that after the second, the tooth had healed six times more slowly than the first time round.

Reiki has proven extremely practical, extremely helpful, and over the years has led to some hilarious encounters too.

One of them happened in a pub in the beautiful seaside town of Brighton, one of my favourite getaway places in the UK. I ordered a meal and found a small table right next to a larger one occupied by a gentleman and his dog. Of course, whenever I see a dog, I have to say hello, so I asked if I could stroke the little fellow, and soon the man and I were engaged in conversation. Inevitably, he asked what I did and I explained I was a Reiki teacher. Then he asked whether I thought Reiki would help with back problems and I replied that I would usually assume it would. It was a night out, and I didn't really want to go much deeper into it. But the universe had other plans.

After a while, a group of the man's friends arrived and we all got talking. Suddenly the guy I had met first made a wrong movement and cried, 'Ouch!' His back was obviously calling for attention. For Reiki. I asked him if he would mind if I helped, then placed my right hand on his lower back. Immediately it felt very warm underneath, so I knew I had found the right spot. We just carried on dining and chatting – me forking my meal with my left hand while I left the other one on the man's back. It was probably the most casual Reiki treatment I have ever given.

One of the people around the table turned out to be a hospital doctor and he had heard of Reiki, which he called an 'application of positive thinking'. I didn't contradict him. I was finding more and more that any attempt to explain Reiki was a lost cause. It needed to be experienced.

My neighbour was experiencing it, and after about 30 minutes I asked him how he felt. He had almost forgotten that he was receiving Reiki! When I took my hand off, he made a few cautious movements, then told everybody, rather incredulously, that the pain had completely gone.

I loved the expression on the doctor's face.

Reiki was also surprisingly useful in everyday life. I used it for even the most ordinary of challenges – my attempts at DIY. When I lived in Germany, I would get my dad to do even the simplest of jobs, like knocking a nail into a wall. In the UK, he was replaced by a handyman, or occasionally a practically-minded friend. To call my DIY skills limited would have been an exaggeration – and suddenly I was doing this sort of thing for a living! Before my first decorating job, I bought a book called *How to Decorate your Flat*, and before more demanding jobs, I consulted Google. But occasionally the smallest jobs proved to be the most difficult.

When I was tasked with replacing curtains with Venetian blinds for every single window in an apartment, for example, I blithely drilled a hole three times the intended size and had to close it with filler and start again. Given that there were another 20 or so holes to go, I felt rather worried. Considering my options, I decided to try something new: giving Reiki to the power drill. Every subsequent hole turned out perfect.

So I started to give Reiki to my printer when it was a bit temperamental, the dishwasher when it stopped working, and eventually my car before I started it. The latter was mainly meant to help with a safe journey, but occasionally it actually had to be used to make the car start.

I also began to give Reiki to important emails before I sent them and even to whole situations. At one stage, I remember driving to work feeling completely overwhelmed by day ahead. I had accepted far too many jobs and there was no way I could complete them all. When I stopped at a traffic light, just for a moment I connected to Reiki and set the intention that it would sort out the problem. I immediately felt my hands getting warm and the energy flowing. Lo and behold, a few minutes later the phone rang and a very apologetic lady asked if it would be at all possible to postpone the work that she had booked for that afternoon. I still remember my utter disbelief. I didn't understand Reiki at all, but that didn't seem to matter. It worked anyway.

But the more I used Reiki, the more puzzling it got. The main reason was that every time it felt different. Although there were similar sensations as well, not one Reiki treatment was exactly like the next, even if I treated the same person several times. And people with similar symptoms could also have different results. Generally, it could be said that if people were in pain, the pain went away. If they had had surgery, they healed much more quickly. But there was another level that made the effects pretty unpredictable – not in a negative way, but in an interesting one.

This, it seemed, had to do with people's life paths. A lot of the differences were due to people having different personalities and being from different backgrounds, at different stages in their lives and in different situations. Step by step, I started to realise that somehow Reiki didn't just play a significant part in people's healing journeys, but also in their journey of self-development.

Given all the amazing experiences I had, I suppose it was all the more puzzling that I found this learning experience often frustrating. I can't deny that in the early days I really struggled to understand why it was so difficult to predict the exact outcome of a Reiki treatment. In fact, I often sat by myself and wondered why I was using something so mysterious. Did I really want to continue with something so unreliable? So inconsistent? As ridiculous as it might sound, I actually started to argue with it. Almost to the point of leaving it behind.

I had been disappointed so many times in my life. So much hadn't worked out. I really didn't want to be disappointed again. I needed something that was steady, reliable, dependable. Presumptuous as it may sound – who was I to make demands? – I decided I would only accept Reiki if it would work for everything, or at the very least be clear as to when and how it would work and when and how it would not. Otherwise, I would give it up.

On reflection, it's probably fair to say that my attitude hasn't changed much. In a way, it's probably become even more extreme. But there's one thing that I've had to accept: if something isn't working the way I want it to work, that doesn't mean it isn't working at all. I just may not have seen the bigger picture.

Which obviously leads to the next question: *is* there a bigger picture? Always? Are all the disasters, disappointments and delays we encounter ultimately for the greater good?

I continued to struggle with this. But one thing kept me going: the simple fact that the sensation in my hands was undeniable. I might not understand it, but it was there.

Of course, I discussed this with Mum all the time. Her advice was to learn more. To take the next Reiki course.

Reiki 1 (for purists, *Shoden*, 'beginner's level' in Japanese) had given me healing hands. Would the next level give me answers?

It did. At least some. But also many more questions.

6.

Next Steps

Around this time, Mum had an experience which still freaks me out when I think of the potential outcome…

My sister had been on a research trip for a film documentary in India and fallen in love. Not just with the country and the food, but also with a guy. For a while she had gone back and forth, and it had become clearer and clearer that this connection would not fade.

However, it wasn't as easy for them to marry as she hoped. First, he didn't have a passport, having never planned to leave India! Secondly, there was the hurdle of obtaining a visa to enter Germany. And that was where they wanted to get married.

As my sister was sounding more and more depressed, I started to wonder whether Reiki could help with the situation. I thought it worth a try. So I connected to Reiki and directed it to my sister overcoming the hurdles standing in the way of her marriage.

To my surprise, images started to appear in my mind. First, I saw paperwork being officially stamped, so I concluded the bridegroom would finally get his passport and visa, and then I saw a wedding, with happy faces, much relief – and a priest conducting the ceremony in a floral garland. That was odd. I remember thinking, 'We don't wear floral garlands in Germany.' It was obvious that I had seen a wedding in India.

I couldn't wait to phone my sister and tell her. She was very relieved about the paperwork, but not convinced about getting married in India. 'All my friends are in Germany,' she said. 'That's definitely where we're going to tie the knot.'

Four months later, they got married. In India.

Mum and I felt really bad about it, because we didn't have the money to join them. After a month of thinking about it, though, we decided that at least one of us had to go. And that would be Mum.

So, off she went, travelling on her own, catching a connecting flight and dragging her suitcase around New Delhi. I was worried about her, but she arrived safely.

The weird thing was that she had been telling me for weeks that she had the strange feeling that something was waiting for her in India. Not just the wedding – something else.

On her last evening there, the newlyweds took her to a restaurant in Pondicherry. But suddenly she didn't feel well. She went to the bathroom and passed out.

Luckily, my sister had followed her. She started shouting, 'Come back! Wake up!' When nothing happened, she finally slapped her.

That did the trick. Mum opened her eyes, quite annoyed. 'What are you doing? Why did I have to come back?'

Later, she told us that when she had passed out, she had been taken on a kind of journey and had entered a large room which was completely filled with people. She couldn't make out their faces, just their silhouettes, but she knew they were familiar. They felt like friends and family. And they were waiting for her.

However there appeared to be something like a pane of glass that prevented her from going over to them. She also noticed a very intense warm light, which she could only describe as sending out love. She wanted to stay in that love.

But it was obviously not her time. When she woke up, she was able to vomit and soon felt better. The next day, it was as if nothing had happened. The only lasting effect was the memory.

I suppose the official term for this is a 'near-death experience'. International research, first published by Raymond Moody in *Life After Life* in 1975, has shown that the majority of people who have been clinically dead, sometimes for a few seconds, sometimes for 20 minutes, and then come back to life report that they have seen a light and people waiting for them. They also often feel surrounded by love. And they all say that they are no longer afraid of death.

The same now applies to Mum, and to me. At least, I am not afraid of my own death. And Mum has promised to hang around for a while.

Hilariously, both Mum and my sister said afterwards they were glad that I hadn't witnessed this event. They thought I would probably have passed out too, or more likely dropped dead right next to Mum.

Back in London, I took Reiki 2 (*Okuden* in Japanese, the 'inner teachings') a few months after the first course. Again it was a weekend course, this time with another teacher. It added new tools and techniques and introduced three Reiki symbols. And that was weird.

Why did Reiki need symbols? For me, a symbol was something secret, almost frightening, something used in secretive lodges. Why should something as open and obvious as Reiki need a secretive element? It didn't help that Reiki students are normally asked not to reveal the symbols to anybody else.

Personally, I have never really obeyed that request, and have even shared the symbols in books and public talks. After all, they are plastered all over the internet, and the worst that can happen if somebody who hasn't been attuned to Reiki draws them is that they won't feel any difference.

Because this is the amazing point: drawing the symbols leads to experiencing energetic vibrations. In other words, they are a short-cut to opening up to higher frequencies. As this was contrary to anything I had previously thought possible, I was gobsmacked. There was no way to deny that these symbols were powerful.

Three symbols form part of the Reiki 2 training and are designed to be used in different situations. The first, often called the Power Symbol, is meant to focus Reiki on physical healing (and the hands tend to feel hotter straight away); the second, the Harmony Symbol, is used for mental and emotional healing; and the third, often referred to as the Connection or Distant Symbol, enables a practitioner to send a Reiki treatment to a person who is not in the same room.

The teacher had the brilliant idea of pairing up the group and asking one of each pair to go to another room. We then 'sent' each other a Reiki treatment. I use this exercise in my Reiki 2 courses to this day. It tends to seal the deal with Reiki.

There was much, much more for me to learn about the symbols, but that took several years. In the meantime, I undertook further training and became a Reiki Master. Not that I particularly felt like one, but at least I learned how to give attunements. That, along with my initial understanding, came to the fore in one of my all-time favourite Reiki experiences, helping Christian.

7.

Christian

Twenty years had passed since I'd last seen my schoolfriend Tanja. We'd just finished school and were about to go our separate ways and head off to university. She became a teacher and found a lovely boyfriend, and we slowly lost touch. So it was something of a surprise when she suddenly got in contact via Facebook. In the meantime, she had married the boyfriend and had three amazing kids. Now she was asking me to visit them when I was next back in Germany.

When I did, I was mesmerised: what a beautiful family! I even joked that I would adopt all of her children. Plus the dog. After that, we stayed in touch regularly via email and phone.

About a year later, I got a very distressing message from her. Just over a week before, she'd been to the premiere of my sister's new film, but her husband hadn't been able to join her because of a cough. Now he had been admitted to hospital. His 'really bad flu' had turned out to be acute leukaemia, and it wasn't looking good at all. When she got in touch, he had been in hospital for about a week. He was receiving the very best care possible, but the outlook was bleak.

Of course Tanja knew that I was practising Reiki. We had talked about it often, but the opportunity had never arisen for her to try it out. Also, I seemed not to have told her that it could be sent over distance. Now she asked if I knew of a practitioner in

Hamburg, or of any other complementary treatments Christian could use while in hospital.

I explained that Reiki could be sent remotely and I'd be very happy to do this for Christian. 'Just ask him to let me know a time and I will connect with him.'

Christian was slightly perplexed. A teacher, an ardent football fan, very much in the here and now, he was what I would call a down-to-earth person. He wouldn't dismiss my more esoteric stories out of hand, but I would certainly get the feeling that he was wondering how much wishful thinking was involved. He liked things to be tangible, practical and 'based on facts'. If they weren't, he would seek a scientific explanation for them. At least that was my impression.

He wasn't against complementary healing, though, and the family had already had amazing experiences with homoeopathy. The idea of healing being sent from the UK to Germany without a physical connection or electronic device would probably be a bit of a stretch for him, but then again, what did he have to lose? He was in hospital, fighting for his life.

So he said, 'Well, if Torsten could send me Reiki at nine o'clock, when all the visitors will have left and I'll be on my own, that would be nice.'

I found out later that he didn't expect anything noticeable to happen, but he liked the idea that somebody somewhere in the world was 'sending positive thoughts' to him.

At half-past nine, he was on the phone to his wife: 'You won't believe what's happened! It was so surreal... I actually *felt* something!'

Tanja told me later that she had rarely heard him so surprised. Or relieved.

He described a sensation almost like gentle electric shocks moving around and even right through his body. And he felt that something positive, something healing and helpful, was going on.

Then he added, 'You know what? For the first time since I was diagnosed, I believe I might actually make it through.'

I carried on sending him Reiki every single night at nine o'clock for the next three months. A few days into these sessions, I suddenly had an intuition: he was going to be home for Christmas. I also felt he wouldn't need a bone marrow or stem cell transplant, contrary to what the doctors had predicted.

It probably sounds like a big commitment to send Reiki every night at nine o'clock for months. In fact, I did have other things to do – primarily, having dinner. Those who know me well tend to mock my habit of having dinner late, mostly around 9 p.m., and the treatments would obviously have clashed with my meal. And I do go out, seeing friends, going to the cinema, even going to the theatre every now and then. Yet I didn't have to sacrifice any of this. I simply *timed* the treatments. As strange as it might sound, Reiki can bridge not only space but time. So whenever I had a 30-minute slot free during the day, I simply sat down, connected to Reiki and gave the treatment, setting the intention for it to be received at 9 p.m. Hamburg time.

Once or twice in fact I was so busy that I actually forgot to send the treatment beforehand. As soon as I remembered, I simply sat down and sent it retrospectively. It still worked. Christian's feedback confirmed it.

But just a few weeks before Christmas, the prognosis was still that if he made it at all, he would have to stay in hospital for many months.

About a week before Christmas, I went to Germany to visit my family there. But first I went to the hospital to see Christian and give him Reiki in person. Then I visited him every day.

While I was in Hamburg, Tanja and I spoke about how helpless she often felt when she visited Christian, not being able to do anything other than support him through her presence. So we decided that it would be a good idea to attune her to Reiki while I was over there. The lack of time didn't allow for a traditional Reiki training, so I introduced her to the basics and gave her a German book on Reiki. I also managed to give her two attunements, and the next day she tried it out on her sister-in-law, who happily confirmed that something was going on. Then she had the confidence to support her husband too.

Three days later, we all left the hospital together. The doctors had declared Christian well enough to spend Christmas at home with his family and then return for further treatment in the new year. I was so excited for him – and I just couldn't believe how accurate my intuition had been! It even prompted me to stray a bit from the usual protocol in Reiki, which is not to pass on any intuitive insights or predictions about certain outcomes. I was so amazed by this confirmation that I told Tanja. And added that I felt he might not even need the bone marrow or stem cell transplant.

Chistian was at home over Christmas and the new year, then was readmitted to hospital and I continued the remote nightly Reiki treatments. Two months later, he had a stem cell transplant. Everything went well, there were no complications and he was declared completely cured. Everybody was relieved and delighted – and so, of course, was I. Yet I still had a nagging question: why had my intuition been telling me that he wouldn't need the transplant?

Back in London, I offered to send the other two Reiki attunements to Tanja remotely. This was a first for me, but I thought I'd give it a try.

For the first one, she duly sat at home at the agreed time and described seeing colours and feeling her palms getting warm, just as you would in an in-person attunement.

The final one was arranged for a Sunday evening at 8 p.m., when she would be home from visiting her husband. But that night she was delayed leaving him and right in the middle of driving home when the attunement was due. The effect was hilarious: suddenly she felt her hands getting warm on the steering wheel. When she stopped at the next traffic light she quickly placed her hands together in *Gassho*, prayer position, the customary Japanese hand position for this ceremony, but of course had to bring them down again when the lights turned green. She then decided (quite rightly) that it would probably work just as well without the hand position, and road safety was more important. When she got home, she was fully attuned. It was this feedback that would eventually give me the confidence to offer online training and distance attunements and reach students all over the world.

A few years later we were driving through Hamburg when suddenly Tanja interrupted the conversation and shouted, 'Here! This is the junction where I got the attunement!'

A few months later I went to Germany again and met up with Christian and his family. As we were sitting in the garden having a barbecue, Tanja took me aside and said that there was something she needed to tell me.

'Do you remember that you told me that Christian might not even need the stem cell transplant?'

'Yes,' I muttered, feeling rather embarrassed.

'Well, actually he was already free of the leukaemia before he had it. The only reason for it was that the doctors found a rare genetic blood disorder as well. They knew if it ever turned cancerous, they wouldn't be able to treat it, so they decided to give him the stem cell transplant as a precautionary measure.'

I still find this the most beautiful Reiki experience I've ever had. If I hadn't already been convinced of the power of Reiki, this surely would have been the final step.

No wonder that when Tanja, Christian and I think of this time, the first word that comes to mind is 'miracle'.

8.

Mastery?

A few months after becoming a Reiki Master, I started to teach my own courses.

It's probably fair to say that I learned more about Reiki from teaching than from any of the courses I'd taken, even though the first one I gave was slightly odd, as I had assembled what was mainly a group of friends, something I never did again, as many came as a favour to me rather than out of a desire to learn Reiki. Still, I had put together everything that I had learned and turned it into what I thought constituted a proper Reiki course. It ticked all the boxes and of course Mum was very proud.

We went for dinner afterwards and discussed how it had gone. There had been more content than I had come across in other courses and it had flowed well. And yet something was missing. Mum knew it. She tried to be as gentle as possible in her criticism, but she was absolutely right. I had taught methods, but not approach. I had taught from the mind, not the heart.

A few weeks later, at the next Reiki 1 course I ran, I summoned up all my courage and started to talk about my own experiences. I talked about my life, the transformation Reiki had brought, the mediumship I had encountered and how I felt that Reiki was somehow linked to spiritual understanding. I added breathing exercises (more on those later) and meditations. The course was an entirely different experience and most students booked for the next level straight away.

Teaching Reiki was definitely the most reassuring decision I ever made. I could see for myself that Reiki wasn't just amazing when *I* was using it – *everybody* could do it! And everybody could get similar results. I couldn't wait for the emails coming in afterwards, detailing all the amazing experiences the students were continuing to have. It was almost unbelievable.

Also, when people came back for the next level, all they wanted to talk about was how their lives had changed. It became obvious that Reiki was a life-changing commodity.

Often, people even left the course in a very different state from how they arrived. Many started off exhausted, unhappy, depressed, burdened with problems. Two days later, they were more relaxed, more confident that they could cope with life and ready to face their problems. None of this was based on wishful thinking, simply on the very tangible experiences they'd already had over the course of the weekend.

It became clearer and clearer that in most cases, the real difference came not through having a Reiki treatment, but through learning Reiki.

One of the most striking examples was a lady called Margot. I'm pleased she has allowed me to use her story in this book.

Margot had emailed me a few weeks before the course, describing her situation: after a recent bereavement, she was struggling to cope with the fallout of a traumatic experience she had had in childhood. She asked me whether I thought that Reiki could help her.

I had learned by then that it wasn't possible to guarantee a particular outcome, but assured her that Reiki would be helpful. How this help would manifest, though, did surprise me.

Margot had first heard about Reiki – or rather, experienced it – a few weeks before, when she had visited a beautician. She must have been looking pretty exhausted and unhappy, because the beautician had spontaneously offered to give her some Reiki after the beauty treatment.

Margot was gobsmacked by the Reiki: she suddenly saw colours and, more importantly, felt loved and calm. This had such an impact that she decided to take it further.

When she arrived at the course, it was obvious that something wasn't quite right. She looked drawn and lost, and was constantly looking down. She also seemed full of fear and extremely tense. Of course, as a teacher, you can see the students' facial expressions and get a pretty good indication of how what you are saying is being received. Seeing the change in Margot's face was just extraordinary. I wish I'd had a camera running and could show it in fast-forward. After the first hour, her expression softened. Then she began to smile, shyly at first, but more confidently as the day went on. She even started to talk to the people sitting around her. By the end of the second day, she was relaxed, smiling broadly and telling everyone how much these two days had already helped her.

But that wasn't the real surprise. She told me later that the week after the course she had gone to the police and reported the person who had sexually abused her over 40 years earlier. Reiki had finally given her the strength to stand up for her rights and prevent anything like that happening again.

She told me she'd been extremely nervous when she turned up at the police station, but the officers had been very understanding and told her, 'If there were more people as brave as you, the world would be a better place.'

This was so contrary to what I had expected that it was a lasting lesson: I realized that healing doesn't necessarily mean letting go; it may mean taking action. We may need to stand up for our rights. And those of other people. Reiki is calming, soothing and relaxing, but also energizing. It inspires us to do the right thing.

It still took a few years for me to realise the true dimension of this: when we are guided by Reiki, we can change the world. At that time, I hadn't taken that step. For me, Reiki was still very much an effective but puzzling individual spiritual healing practice. But, like my students, I was learning.

Other students experienced physical healing, often even at the courses. One lady limped into a workshop, having twisted her ankle the previous day, and asked if it was okay to take some painkillers. Would this hinder the flow of Reiki? I told her I didn't think it would be a problem, but if she could bear to wait a few minutes, we could ask some students to give her Reiki. Fifteen minutes later, the pain was gone, and she easily managed to get through the day without any painkillers.

In a much more serious position were three students who all suffered from Crohn's disease. They had all undergone surgery, some of them more than once, and it had severely impaired their everyday life. One lady almost couldn't eat unless she was in the bathroom at the same time, because her body didn't process her food at all, but let it pass through straight away. After the Reiki course, her condition significantly improved. The following week she sent me an email saying that she just had her first breakfast that had actually stayed in her body.

Another student, a man in his forties who suffered from the same disease and had been off work for over a year, was able to return to normal life afterwards. Subsequently, he decided to change his career and is now promoting well-being and positivity and helping people to find the job that is their real calling.

The third student suffering from Crohn's disease, a lady in her thirties, was on heavy medication when she started with Reiki. Over the years, the disease had restricted her so much that even her marriage hadn't survived. She began to use Reiki daily on herself, and after a few weeks felt so much better that she went to see her specialist and asked whether it would be okay to pause the medication. Being well aware of the damaging side-effects of the drugs, he agreed it was worth a try and advised her that she could stop one of them straight away and begin to phase the other one out. Should the symptoms come back, she'd be put on the medication again. Today she is a Reiki Master and has never had to go back on either medication.

But the more people I taught, the more I realized how fluid life was and how difficult it could be: happy relationships, unhappy relationships; successful careers, unsuccessful careers; rewarding ones, unfulfilling ones; physical problems; psychological challenges; traumatic experiences; times of happiness, times of struggle. For all the help that Reiki could give, I struggled with why there was so much unhappiness in the world in the first place. Even moments of happiness often seemed to be set against a backdrop of challenges.

This affected me so much I could only watch a movie once I had been assured it had a happy ending. I haven't seen *Titanic* to this day...

The beautiful feedback from Reiki courses and treatments, though, were encouraging. The stories above are just a tiny selection, but they are representative.

Then my journey changed dramatically with one student, Jason.

9.

Jason

The most important lesson I ever received through Reiki came in my first year of teaching it, and much was still in development, not least my trust in the system. It would change not only my understanding of Reiki, but also my understanding of life.

A married couple booked onto a Reiki 1 course. They were only in their mid-thirties, but the husband, Jason, had just been diagnosed with skin cancer and told he had eight weeks to live. They lived abroad, but he was being treated at a specialist hospital in London, so they came over regularly.

Straight after the diagnosis, they had researched as much as they could about the therapies available and found evidence that complementary therapies helped cancer patients to live longer. Jason had searched the internet for a suitable therapy and decided on Reiki.

After their Reiki attunements, they were quite baffled by the fact that they could physically feel something, but they enjoyed the spiritual reflections that were by then an integral part of my courses. At the end of the weekend, we had a drink together at the pub around the corner and became good friends. A few weeks later, they booked onto Reiki 2.

Over the following months, I met their lovely children and visited Jason whenever he was in London to give him Reiki treatments. Sometimes we went out for dinner afterwards, but after a few months this became too difficult for him and he stayed at home.

That was the odd thing: I gave him Reiki treatments, he received treatments from his wife and he also used Reiki on himself; he loved the sessions, he talked about the visions and experiences he had, and he found more and more calm and peace; and the sessions also helped him to recover after the surgery. But he still *needed* the surgery. More and more of it. The cancer spread and spread. Every time I saw him, more tumours had developed: in his spine, his neck, his brain. At one point he needed a walking stick, a few months later a wheelchair.

And yet, the longer this went on, the more peaceful he became. He accepted his fate.

I didn't. Every time I gave him a treatment, in person or remotely, I hoped that the cancer would go into remission. Or at least stop spreading. With the opposite happening, I sincerely began to question what I was doing.

What kept me going were the conversations we had after the treatments – conversations about the spiritual connection he felt and the meaning of the colours and symbols he saw. For an out-and-out technical person, a highly trained computer specialist in the financial sector, this was certainly unusual. At least, Jason said it was. He had never entertained the thought of anything alternative, esoteric or spiritual before. Now it was his new normal.

Just under a year later, I received a request from his wife to send him distance Reiki. He hadn't been able to travel to London for a while and had just been admitted to the local hospital. The doctors only gave him a few more days.

Of course, I sent him a Reiki treatment straight away. What I felt was so strong and powerful, though, that I doubted the end was near. It felt to me that a proper fight against the cancer was going on, rather than a surrender to it.

But when I sent him another treatment the next day, I felt nothing. The following week I received an email telling me that he had passed that day.

I felt like a complete failure.

Why hadn't the Reiki worked? Why did he have to die? Almost, at least energetically, in my arms!

A few weeks later, I heard from his wife again. She told me that the day before his death he had indeed had a sudden surge of energy, mirroring what I had felt. It was as if everything within him had made one last attempt to stay on Earth. But the next day, the energy was gone.

She also told me something else: a few days before, when it had become clear to both of them that he didn't have much time left, they had said goodbye to each other. Only he hadn't said goodbye, he'd said, 'I'll see you on the other side.'

I suddenly realised that Reiki had given Jason – and his entire family – the greatest healing possible: the awareness that life doesn't end with death.

A few weeks later, I went away for a few days, and the story took another turn. I had planned to hole up in a nice little hotel by the seaside to work on a project, and Mum had picked an angel card for me that stated 'Retreat', so, reassured that I was doing the right thing, I drove down to Torquay. (I find the guidance of cards is often amazing!)

The hotel, however, was awful. If you have ever watched the English comedy series *Fawlty Towers*, which was actually inspired by a hotel in Torquay, you'll get the picture. Although most of the hotel was empty, they gave me the smallest ground floor room possible, with a window set so high that I could barely look out. And when I did, I saw nothing but a grim car park. The fact that the heating was switched off for several hours during the day (I had planned to stay indoors most of the time and work), the wi-fi patchy and the pool closed just added to the misery. Why on Earth had I been guided to this hotel?

And I *had* been guided: I had asked Reiki to help me choose the right hotel before I made the booking.

In the evening I decided to have a drink in the hotel bar, the only welcoming place in the building, and started talking to a man I took to be a fellow guest. It turned out that he wasn't actually staying at the hotel, having had a bad experience there previously, but had just dropped in to have a drink. We had an amazing conversation, starting with music and pets and ending with Reiki and spirituality. Seeing my interest, he highly recommended a visit to the town's Spiritualist church. And he kindly gave me the name of a better hotel too.

The next day, I moved to a much friendlier place with a beautiful view and staff I am friends with to this day.

Two days later, I visited the Spiritualist church. At weekends, they hosted psychic mediums for platform appearances. In other words, the medium would stand on a platform at the front of the room and give messages to members of the audience. Even though I didn't receive one myself, I was surprised by the detail and accuracy of the medium I saw.

The programme for the rest of the month brought another surprise: the following week's speaker was Keith Hall, the very medium I had seen all those years earlier during my bankruptcy. I extended my stay by another week and saw him on stage. Again, he was mind-blowingly accurate. Afterwards, I said hello and asked whether he also gave private readings. He invited me to his home the next day.

When I visited him in his tiny Victorian cottage, the first thing he said was: 'There is a young man coming in who wants to say hello. He must be in his thirties and tells me that he passed just a few weeks ago... I hear the word "cancer".'

Then he paused for a moment and asked, 'Does the name "Jason" mean anything to you?'

When he saw tears coming into my eyes, he gently added, 'He just wants to say thank you for the help you gave him.'

My teaching changed significantly after this. I realised I could give answers and explanations on a very different level. And Keith became a good friend for many years.

When he passed away, a few weeks after I started work on this book, I found it rather hard to accept that he wasn't meant to see its publication. I'm certain he would have been inundated with requests for private readings and I would have been so happy for him to finally gain the recognition I felt he deserved. Instead, he decided to pass it on to the younger generation.

I had made plans to go out for the evening in London when I got the message that Keith had died. I couldn't return the ticket for the club, so decided to go anyway and just take things a bit more quietly.

It turned out to not be as quiet as planned and I met a very good-looking guy who made it clear that he was interested in me. We spent the rest of the evening together, and after a while he asked me what I did for a living. When he heard the word *Reiki*, his eyes suddenly got even brighter, and, assuming that I would have an understanding of this kind of stuff, he told me that he was about to train as a psychic medium.

All I could think of was to go within and ask Keith, 'Did you arrange this?'

I got an image of him with a big smile.

10.

Another Passing

Around the time I met Jason, I had another strange experience. I sometimes wonder if I was meant to have these experiences early on, so I wouldn't see Reiki as just a complementary therapy. But I can't deny that life was really getting a bit weird...

A young lady, probably in her late twenties, booked on a course together with two girlfriends. She had arranged everything for the group, but in the end she herself didn't turn up. When the other two arrived, they explained that a friend of hers had had an accident.

A few days later, she emailed me and asked if I would be able to visit her friend in hospital. A young man around her age, who, I guessed, she quite fancied, had sustained a knee injury doing sports. It turned out that an operation wasn't needed and he just required a few days' rest. Unbeknownst to anyone, though, a blood clot had formed, and it moved around his body to his brain, where it blocked an artery. When I arrived at the hospital, he had been in a coma for a week.

I met the young lady there and we went to the intensive care unit, where the young man was connected to an enormous number of machines and monitors, and asked a nurse if it was okay to give him a Reiki treatment. She had no objections, and I confirmed that I wouldn't physically touch him. I sat down next to him and connected to Reiki.

Nothing happened. Reiki wouldn't flow.

I tried everything: deep breathing to open up more, the Power Symbol to feel Reiki more strongly, intention, surrender, whatever I could think of. Even the Connection Symbol didn't establish a connection. Or did it? Because when I looked up, I suddenly *saw* something. About 12 inches above the young man's body, there was an amorphous lime green shape.

It was mesmerising. And I knew it was that guy. Outside his body. Was I seeing his soul?

It still wouldn't take Reiki, but somehow I realised it wasn't needed. It was designed to be used in this realm, and this young guy wasn't fully part of it anymore. I felt he hadn't decided whether to stay on Earth or not. Moving to the next level would mean leaving many devastated people behind. But returning to his body would probably mean dealing with severe impairment for the rest of his life. I had the strong feeling that he was in the process of making his decision and already half in the spirit realm, so beyond our influence.

I asked his friend, together with another girl from their circle who had just arrived, whether they followed any religion. Both were Indian, and they confirmed what I had hoped for – that they had been raised in the Hindu tradition. Not that it ultimately mattered, but it made the situation easier to explain.

Luckily, the two young ladies found my explanation helpful. It freed them from any responsibility. Whatever happened would be the right thing for him on the soul level.

They told me that his mother in India had been informed and was on her way over to see him. In the end, it appeared he decided to hang on so that she could see him and say goodbye. He passed away the day after her arrival.

His friend took up Reiki soon afterwards.

There were also interesting experiences on the courses I was teaching, to the point where the weird became the normal.

At that time I used to place three photographs next to me when I was teaching. I had been told that it was an Eastern tradition to have a picture of the founder of your spiritual tradition or your own teacher near you to remind you to teach with respect. So, many Reiki teachers would put pictures of Mikao Usui, the Reiki founder, and two of his successors, Chujiro Hayashi and Hawayo Takata, in the room, and I did too.

I was usually careful to take these pictures with me when I was teaching, only one weekend I forgot. One of the students on that course had psychic abilities and asked me during the break whether I was aware that I had a guide. At the time, I wasn't really sure, so I just asked her if she had become aware of anyone. She said she had, and described an oriental man standing behind me.

Rectifying my mistake, the next day I took the pictures of the early Reiki teachers with me and placed them where they normally stood. When the psychic student came in, to my astonishment she pointed straight to the picture of Mikao Usui and said, 'That's the guy I saw behind you yesterday.'

Today, I don't take these pictures on my courses anymore. It feels a bit too much like a cult of personality. Reiki isn't about particular people, it's about universal connection. But the early masters are obviously still involved, and Mikao Usui would have a pivotal role to play in my life later on.

11.

Mum and I

By now it has probably become patently obvious that Mum has also played a major role in my life.

I never really thought twice about this. I just took it for granted. We were obviously soulmates – we had similar tastes, ideas and aspirations, a similar approach to life, and we enjoyed each other's company. And when we shared a house in London, we saw each other every day.

To explain things a bit more, let me go back to a time before the bankruptcy, before I had ever heard of Reiki, before I even knew how to spell the word 'karma'. To a time when my sister passed on the email address of a German lady called Monika, who was in the strange business of offering online 'channellings'. All you had to do was to send her an email asking for one. How very odd.

'Hello, my name is Torsten. Can I please have a channelling?'

The reply came almost straight away: 'Sure, please transfer 30 euros into my account and let me know if you have any questions. Otherwise, we'll just see what comes.'

I thought that was remarkably reasonable, paid the fee and told her I just wanted a general reading. Not entirely trusting the process, I didn't want to give her any clues through my questions!

A week later, the email with the channelling arrived. Despite the rather odd language, the content was mind-blowing:

My beloved child of the starry sky,

We here in the kingdom of light see your growth and the work you do during the day with admiration.

In this life you have decided to help and support your mother, although sometimes you want to throw in the towel.

But this is quite normal.

Sometimes, when you have time to think, you are reminded that you would like to live a life without obligations, without coercion, without any responsibility.

But these thoughts only come up for a short time, because actually you still want to achieve very, very much in your soul, and you know that this is associated with a lot of work.

You have a mother who is very close to your heart. You are both very connected and very similar in your soul.

You have inherited a lot of character traits from her – the ambition, the slight obsessiveness, the perseverance and the strength to get things done.

You feel a great connection to and love for her.

We want to show you what you're up to in order to convey a better understanding to you.

Listen carefully to what we are ready to tell you:

You lived in a faraway land many, many years ago.

You were a ship-builder.

You worked for the rich.

You yourself came from a poor family, but you worked your way up and were promoted by rich, powerful people because you were so beautiful to look at.

You also had a special talent, namely singing.

You had a voice as clear as a bell, so people became aware of you and listened to you.

Your appearance – blond with blue eyes – opened the gates to the world of the rich and powerful.

You sang at many events and were applauded and cheered.

At the same time, you experienced a lot of bad things. Because you had such a pretty face, many men were after you. They circled you like maggots around bacon.

You could not escape them and so you were abused by them and used for their purposes.

At first you hated it, but over time you got used to it and capitalized on your looks.

As a little boy it was a big, difficult learning process for you, but you handled it very well and thereby reduced a lot of karma.

You got to know a rich patron who loved you very much and gave you all his money.

He was many years older than you, but you felt a certain kind of love for him because he was good to you.

This man fulfilled all your wishes and made it possible for you to have an apprenticeship.

You chose to become a builder of ships.

In your soul you were very ambivalent, because on the one hand you were attracted to women, but on the other hand you were also drawn to the male sex, because you hadn't known anything else since childhood.

When you were in a country surrounded by sea and cliffs, you met a woman who asked you to transport goods on your ships – silks, fabrics and the like.

You stood face to face, and for the first time in your life, you felt love for a woman, and you were amazed.

That woman is your mother in this life.

You have a very good relationship with her, since once you led a life together in love and light.

You have lived through everything together, and that is why you have decided to come back to Earth again: to put a project back on its feet and to accompany her with love.

You have made a conscious decision to take on this role because it allows you to be close to each other.

Your mother is full of power, as are you.

Neither of you is keen on forming another solid partnership, since you have each other. And it is more important for both of you to pursue your goals and to achieve them.

You just want to accomplish what you set out to do.

Only when this is done will you both get involved in a relationship with a new partner. For now, you have put everything else on the back-burner.

Hence this kind of mutual obsession.

When you have achieved your goal, you and your mother will almost simultaneously enter into a marriage and start a new life.

However, this partnership will not take place in Germany – you will get married in another country and stay there.

You will lose sight of Germany completely. It was never your true home. In your heart you always wanted to go into the big wide world.

You have already suffered a loss here on Earth that your soul is still dealing with.

Believe me, my son, we love you very much here and you will soon be rewarded for your hard work and your natural kindness.

You have a great understanding of the needs of poor people because you still have your previous life in mind, and that's why we value you very much.

We are now sending you the angel of love and enlightenment. He is now above you.

While reading these lines, let the pure, true love of God flow into every cell of your soul, into every fibre of your being.

This love and the light that is now in you will help you to achieve your goals and to spend your life in love and light here on Earth.

You are very fortunate to be able to be here on Earth with your mother, because you come from the same soul family and are so similar in every way.

Even if there is occasional friction, you have never been really angry with each other and never will be, because your love for each other is as pure and as deep as the eternal ocean.

Your mother will always give you her love. She will always keep it ready for you when you are worried. She is always on your side.

We are happy for you, because the good times are only just beginning.

The hard struggle of work will soon be over and you will be able to reap the fruits of your labour.

You are a fighter, you fight the fight of the righteous, and for this you have our blessing.

Great, great love and gratitude, for you are a little angel on Earth who came here to work.

Deep love.

My name is ELIAS.

Here in the kingdom of light you are called Allsonus, the benevolent.

Greetings from God.

Wow! This certainly wasn't what I expected. For all I knew, it could all be true. But I didn't quite understand what I was supposed to do with the information … This was before I had learned Reiki and I remember thinking, 'How do you bring goodness into the world with jewellery designs?' And having met Mum in another life was also a bit much to take in. After all, there was no way to get independent proof…

On the other hand, it was remarkable that this lady in Bavaria had singled out the most unusual feature of my life – my closeness to Mum. But of course I couldn't just go around telling people that my mum had actually been my wife in a previous life. So for well over a decade, I kept this channelling to myself.

The email is still in my inbox and of course I printed it out too. But it took me years to realise its true meaning.

Meanwhile, Mum and I explored life together. We even tried to do yoga together, but this was, at least on her side, rather short-lived. For a lady in her mid-sixties, with osteoporosis setting in, it wasn't the perfect modality. But I loved it!

I also found the similarities to Reiki quite remarkable. One is often referred to as a complementary therapy, the other as a series of stretching exercises, and both descriptions fall so very short.

Surprisingly few yoga classes seem to teach what the word actually means. Instead, the focus is placed on increased physical strength and suppleness and reduced stress. Or on controlling body and mind through breathing and exercises. Okay, I really loved the headstand! But what is often forgotten is that these exercises are the means to an end. Yes, they promote relaxation and suppleness and strengthen the core, but these are steps on the path to the ultimate destination: union. That is what the word 'yoga' means: the union between Atman and Brahman, which basically means the union between individual and divine consciousness. Yoga is a path to realising oneness.

For me, the most unexpected part of the physical practice turned out to be the breathing exercises. The power of deep abdominal breathing took me so much by surprise that I started to incorporate it into my Reiki classes. It was only much later that I learned that the technique was a basic exercise in the original Japanese Reiki teachings. It even had a Japanese name, *Joshin Kokyo-Ho*.

I started to take workshops in yogic philosophy and was amazed to find so much relevance in the ancient scriptures of the Bhagavad Gita and the Vedic philosophy of the Upanishads. They made a lot of sense. Why wasn't all this in Reiki?

In the end, I gave my entire family a crash course on yoga for Christmas.

Yoga also led, in a rather curious way, to exploring a technique that turned out to become the second pillar in my spiritual understanding: past-life regression.

A few weeks after I started yoga, I booked myself on an intensive four-day retreat with exercise sessions morning, noon and night. My body clearly wasn't ready for this, and on the second day I developed symptoms of sciatica. Luckily, as I later discovered, they weren't actually caused by a trapped nerve – I had simply over-exercised the muscles in that area – but the pain was still excruciating.

I almost left the retreat, but ultimately managed to reduce the pain to a manageable level. As taking part in the exercises was now out of the question, I had a browse through the small bookshop at the retreat centre. And one book caught my eye.

Students often tell me the same thing: a book suddenly stands out, or even falls off the shelf in front of them, and they know they need to read it. That happened to me. I *had* to read that book. By the end of the retreat, I'd almost finished it.

The book was *Many Lives, Many Masters* by an American psychiatrist called Brian Weiss. Mum read it, too, and we were both fascinated. The idea of past lives had already been implanted in my mind by *Conversations with God* and by the channelling from Monika. But it hadn't quite occurred to me that information about past lives could be directly accessed in this one. And you could do it yourself.

To be honest, I had already had some Reiki clients who had memories that clearly weren't from their current incarnation. But they were often just short glimpses and seemed quite different from the clarity of the memories described by Brian Weiss.

He described a simple method that made it possible to access past-life memories in a hypnotherapy session. A week later I found a lady in London offering just that and booked myself in. I had been to a hypnosis workshop before, and after several unsuccessful attempts to shift my awareness, the hypnotherapist had decided that I was unhypnotisable, but I still thought it was worth a try.

I listened to the soothing voice of the therapist telling me to relax … and I did slowly relax. At one point she accidentally dropped of a bottle of lavender oil into the diffuser, which caused me to have a coughing fit, but not even that stopped me from relaxing, while remaining fully aware of the therapist's voice, the room temperature and my own breathing and comfort.

After a while, the therapist asked, 'What are you seeing?'

Frankly, not much. Just some bubbles floating around. Rather embarrassed, I told her about it. I was pretty certain it meant the regression wouldn't work for me and she'd have to give up.

But she just said, 'Step into one of those bubbles – they contain your past lives.'

'Huh?' I thought. 'How do I step into a bubble?'

But I didn't want to ask, so I just used my intention – and suddenly found myself *inside* one. Well, *I* wasn't inside exactly, but the Hollywood actress Elizabeth Taylor was. How ridiculous! And how typical. What I saw was Elizabeth Taylor in her most famous role as Cleopatra – the very image that people use to make fun of past lives, saying that people were always either Julius Caesar, Napoleon or another famous person plucked out of world history. Now, I was Cleopatra, and not even that – I was Elizabeth Taylor *playing* Cleopatra. This must be my stupid imagination.

But somehow I was really inside the scene, and when I started to look around, I noticed that although the woman in front of me did bear striking resemblance to Elizabeth Taylor's Cleopatra, on closer inspection she looked a bit different. Also, she wasn't in an Egyptian palace, but a temple with ancient Greek-style columns, surrounded by what looked like a desert, so possibly slightly further south than Greece. She was performing some rituals, nervously looking to the left and the right, as if making sure that nobody was watching. As a woman, would she have been allowed to do that?

Then what looked like a large vase or amphora fell over, spilling grains all over the floor. I suppose it must have been an offering at the temple.

The lady was so shocked, she immediately got up and ran away.

Then there was a cut, and when the film-like scene continued, it was several decades later. The same lady, looking much older now, was sitting in a very basic shelter, surrounded by people who were listening to her as she explained the deeper meaning of life. She had become a spiritual teacher.

I can't say that I was 100 per cent convinced that this was truly a past-life experience, and the session was more expensive than anything I had ever come across in the field of complementary therapies, so when I woke up again, I thought, 'Okay, that was quite interesting, but it was really a lot of money for only 20 minutes.'

When I checked my watch, though, it turned out that almost two hours had passed! I had obviously lost complete track of time.

Before we had started, the regression therapist had asked me to set the intention of seeing a past life that was significant for my current one. Was this scene repeating itself in my current life? Was I running away from something?

I didn't know. It had been an interesting experience, but I couldn't say that it was mind-blowing. Certainly not life-changing. I discussed it with Mum, then put it to the back of my mind.

12.

'I Don't Want This!'

Soon after I became a Reiki Master, I went through a crisis. I'd already had an amazing range of Reiki experiences, so it is surprising how little I had accepted my path. On one hand, I loved teaching the courses and going deeper into Reiki. But on the other, I missed my old life.

At weekends, I was teaching; during the week, I was cleaning carpets and decorating houses. This wasn't the life I wanted – not at all. I didn't want to wear myself out with all the physical work, but I didn't just want to do Reiki either, even though that side of my life was becoming more and more successful. By now I had founded the Reiki Academy London and the courses were filling up quickly, often through recommendations.

But they had become so deeply spiritual that it was becoming a problem, because I didn't want the role of a spiritual teacher, or what I associated with it. I didn't want to meditate all day long, live in basic surroundings and not have a private life. That was how the swamis in my yoga centre lived, and I thought that was what was expected. But I had a passion for politics, loved art and the theatre, and really enjoyed good food and wine. And I wanted to build a business and be successful enough to afford a nice house for myself and Mum. I was convinced that none of this would be compatible with the path of a spiritual teacher.

I felt like Whoopi Goldberg in *Call Me Claus*, not wanting to become Santa Claus, even though the white beard was already growing.

I was fighting the universe and myself. Not a good combination of adversaries.

Of course, this didn't escape Mum. It worried her. She knew I was on the path that was right for me, but how to keep me on it? She decided to Google Brian Weiss.

I still remember how excited she was when she came downstairs to tell me that she had found out that he was actually teaching past-life regression therapy. Normally the prerequisites were to be a hypnotherapist or psychotherapist, but some other therapists would also be accepted. Surely a Reiki Master should be eligible!

Specifically, Brian Weiss was teaching two courses a year in upstate New York and they were normally booked up months in advance.

Mum looked at me meaningfully.

I tried to argue that life was too uncertain to make plans half a year ahead, that it would be far too expensive and that I couldn't really take two weeks off my property work.

All Mum said was, 'If you are meant to be there, the universe will make it possible.' And she made sure I reserved my place. A few weeks later, the course was full, so that was a smart move.

Putting all my trust in the universe, I then did something I had previously said I would never do again: I took out a bank loan – and booked my flight.

I wasn't planning on learning past-life regression for use on others; I merely wanted to find out more about myself. Mainly, why I was struggling to accept my path.

And I did get some clues. Two regressions in particular were worth the journey on their own.

The first was part of a group exercise, with Brian Weiss' voice guiding us from the front. I hadn't expected this simple technique to work for a group of 150 people at once, but duly closed my eyes and a few minutes later found myself in a medieval market square on some kind of stage or pedestal, speaking to a crowd.

The dress of the people was European and I had the feeling that I was in the south of France. There was a lot of tension, a lot of nervousness, a lot of demands for change. And that seems to have been what my speech was all about: social change and the rights of individuals. I wouldn't say it was very spiritual – it felt far more political. But it was driven by the idea of improving living conditions for all.

What was particularly interesting was that the market square was literally a square shape, just like the little town, as can still be seen in the Cathar region of France. The style of buildings and clothing indicated the 14th or 15th century AD and I seem to have been some kind of political activist, travelling from town to town trying to inspire people to stand up for their rights.

For some reason, though, it didn't work out. At some stage in the regression, I fast-forwarded to a later stage in that life, when I was an old man. Quite a few years must have passed, and I was revisiting one of the towns I had spoken in before. Nobody paid any attention to me now. Nobody was interested in change. Nobody had taken the advice that I had given.

I stayed with an old supporter, now a good friend, and we talked about the time when we had had high ideals and how the world had moved on and our efforts had come to nothing. Instead of inspiration and progress, there was resignation and stagnation. People were so focused on their individual struggles that they had no energy to think of society as a whole.

One of the techniques that Brian Weiss suggested was to ask yourself at the end of the regression what you might have learned in that life. As soon as I did that, I heard: 'You can't change others. You can only change yourself.'

My mood was sombre... My ideas hadn't caught fire as I'd hoped. Nothing had changed. Was I afraid of this in my current life? Was I afraid of disappointment?

What was interesting was my connection with France... I'd taught my first two Reiki Master courses there – not far from towns with square marketplaces, in fact – and a French publisher had brought out the first foreign language edition of my first Reiki book.

The second, more impactful regression also took me to France. This time, it was facilitated by fellow students in an exercise where we were asked to group up to try regressions ourselves. I had become friends with two lovely American ladies who decided to try to regress me.

I lay down on some cushions at the side of the large teaching hall with several regressions going on around me – not the perfect backdrop for going into a place of stillness. Then, a few minutes into the regression, the two ladies suddenly started to giggle. The more they tried to suppress it, the worse it got. They just couldn't help themselves and thought they had completely messed things up, but instead, the opposite happened. Of course, I noticed both the giggling and the efforts to contain it, but, remarkably, I was somehow able to distinguish between the outside world and the journey I was on in my mind. That seems to be a typical sign of being in a hypnotic state. But where was I?

What I saw was a relatively young man, probably around 30, in a remote location. He – or rather, I – was surrounded by a group of people, about 20 or 30 of them, mostly young men. Oddly, it seems that I was something like a spiritual teacher once more. The content was somehow connected to the teachings of Jesus, but not as they are traditionally taught in churches. It sounded more radical and more encompassing. And it was about personal development.

The people were listening carefully to every word I said and they had started to look at life in a different way. They were ready to leave everything behind and live a life of meditation and celibacy. But somehow that didn't feel right to me. It didn't feel right that they should leave behind their families, their jobs and their normal lives and go into the wilderness and live a monastic life rather than bring their spiritual understanding into their everyday life.

This meeting was a big turning-point. Many seemed to have followed me for a long time, and now I just sent them back. I could see by their faces that they were shocked, but they eventually accepted it, and I was left standing there by myself. I had realised that I had taken the responsibility for their lives upon myself and that this would deny them the chance to develop. To become the change-makers they could be.

The biggest surprise came when I went back to my childhood in that life. It was the exact same family that I have in my current incarnation. They had some kind of farm then and worked really hard. I could clearly see their exhaustion. My sister was supporting them, doing lots of manual work. I didn't have to – I didn't have to play my part at all. Somehow, they all knew what I was going to do later on. Not that I was being groomed for it – I didn't seem to have a teacher, I was merely given the space to develop. While they were working hard to feed the family, I was sitting by a pond, meditating.

As surreal, almost unbelievable, as these regressions felt, they somehow did the trick: I accepted that I didn't have to repeat those experiences, but could move on and be a spiritual teacher while leading a normal life.

Combining a personal spiritual journey with the demands of everyday life seems to be a problem many people face. But our entire life, every single mundane aspect of it, is part of our spiritual journey.

I realised I had a job to do. And to my surprise, I began to enjoy it.

I probably didn't need to travel all the way to the USA to find this out, but I was a hard nut to crack, so maybe there was no other way after all. And, as a side-effect, I learned how to facilitate past-life regressions myself.

13.

Independent Proof

I began to offer past-life workshops to my students and was amazed by the experiences they shared. Three regressions were so outstanding that I had no doubt that these memories were real rather than just figments of the imagination.

One happened in a workshop where I offered a new technique that I had learned from Brian Weiss. The students had to pair up, look into each other's eyes and say, 'I see you as....' Then they would describe what they saw. Two ladies, both in their thirties, who had never met before, worked together on that exercise and one started to describe the other as a soldier in World War II, dying from a gunshot wound.

Of course, it's easy to say that this is pretty general. After all, there were millions of soldiers in that war, and many would have died from a gunshot wound. But the description became more and more detailed and the lady explained that the bullet had come from a particular angle that had created a wound stretching all the way from the soldier's right hip to the beginning of his rib cage.

The lady receiving this information was normally very chatty and bubbly, but became quieter and quieter during the exercise. After a few weeks she had finally digested it enough to share with me why it resonated with her so much: she had a birthmark on the right side of her body, stretching all the way from her right hip to her rib cage – exactly where the other lady had seen the gunshot wound! Of course, the birthmark had been covered by layers of clothing during the regression exercise.

Another fascinating example came from a retreat I ran in Spain. One of the organisers took part in the regression and saw herself as a 'white witch' in England. She was persecuted and had to flee to Scotland, where she was eventually killed.

During the regression, when I asked whether the participants could detect a date, the year 1563 came into her mind straight away. Of course, as soon as the regression was over, she took out her mobile and Googled '1563 witchcraft'. To her utter amazement, it was the very year that Parliament had passed an 'Act agaynst Conjuracons, Inchantments and Witchecraftes' – witchcraft was outlawed in England and persecution began.

In her current life, she brings spiritual speakers to huge audiences and plays an important role in facilitating a wider understanding of the many different spiritual paths on offer.

Mum had an interesting past-life regression too. Unsurprisingly, just like me, she was taken to a life in medieval France. She lived in a castle and described some of the architectural elements that stood out for her. She was surprised by the strange shape of the windows, which were narrow and ended in an arch. But not at the top, as you would expect, but at the bottom. She also described the particular shape of the roofs of the turrets on the castle.

Later, she was a student on my first Reiki Master course, which I offered at a rural retreat centre near Carcassonne in southern

France. I added a day for excursions, and when we visited the ruins of a medieval Cathar castle, Mum suddenly stood and stared. She couldn't believe what she was seeing: a whole series of narrow windows with the arch not at the top, but at the base.

Later, when we drove to Carcassonne, Mum looked at the immaculately preserved city walls and said, 'Something isn't right here. The roofs on the turrets are the wrong shape.' She had no idea that the city had been rebuilt by a history enthusiast in the 19th century, by which time it had been in such a poor state that he'd had to imagine parts of the design. Subsequently, art historians had pointed out that the shape of the turret roofs was wrong.

These are the kind of stories you simply couldn't make up. And of course, when we ponder the idea of past lives a bit further, it leads to some interesting questions. Could it be that our current incarnation is determined by a previous one? Or even several? How much of our current life is the result of karma that has built up over previous lives? And, if our lives are designed for us to learn, what are we supposed to learn in our current one?

Together with my experiences of mediumship and the tangible connection to deeper levels of existence that we can experience in Reiki, these past-life regressions instilled in me the unshakable conviction that we come back ... again and again.

This current life is just one of many. And of course, this brings a completely different take on life, its challenges and experiences.

Somewhere along the way, my Reiki teaching had changed. It had become clearer and more confident. I had realised that Reiki was so much more than I had originally thought.

It had also become clear that I didn't have to add any spiritual insights from other traditions. They were all somehow already in Reiki. I just hadn't seen it.

A second Master course, taken with another teacher, brought a better understanding of the Japanese origins of the system, but also a new problem: it got too Japanese for me. It became apparent that you could get so absorbed in Japanese traditions that the universal principles of Reiki became obscured.

Essentially, my own courses became based around the understanding that life can only be understood through the lens of reincarnation and that Reiki is a tool to connect to these higher eternal realms of existence. And I felt that it was time to sum it up in a book.

When most of it was written, I sent the manuscript to a publishing house. After a rather agonizing wait, eventually an email came back asking me to arrange a phone call. Would they be interested?

They weren't. The editor explained that she thought it was a good book, but too personal for somebody who wasn't already known. She wished me all the best.

Once I got over my frustration, I finished the manuscript and was just about to self-publish, so that at least my students could read it, when I received a phone call from the same editor. They were about to publish an introductory series to different spiritual topics – did I want to put together a proposal for the book on

Reiki? Six months later, my first book was published: an introduction to Reiki.

Suddenly, pretty much everything was in place: the Reiki Academy London was thriving and now I had a book on Reiki published by a well-known publishing house.

Time to spruce up my website. I didn't want to change the look much, but thought it would be nice to add a few images from Japan, for example the memorial stone erected in honour of the Reiki founder and the mountain where Reiki was first experienced.

As I didn't want to steal them from the internet, I asked a few Reiki teachers who had been to Japan if they had any pictures I could use. But either they didn't write back at all or they explained that their publishers or website hosts owned the image rights.

That left only one option: taking some pictures myself.

A week later, I booked a flight to Japan.

Looking back, I find it interesting how I had been resisting the idea of connecting Reiki with Japan. After all, it was obvious that it originated there. The name was Japanese, the founder was Japanese and many of its techniques were clearly rooted in Japanese martial arts and spiritual traditions. Given that my whole approach to Reiki had been to excavate the original teachings, my reluctance to embrace Japan was a complete contradiction.

But there was a reason for it: I thought that something as powerful and deep as Reiki should be accessible from anywhere and work for anyone, as of course is the case. If a certain location or ethnicity were particularly conducive to its use, it would be promoting separation, not connection. And it didn't feel right to focus on a particular culture when using a universal healing system. After all, the first syllable of Reiki is often translated as 'universal'.

And there was another problem: religion. Reiki is generally regarded as a system that can work with any personal belief system. It is all about experiencing energy and healing, not about imposing a particular faith. Mikao Usui made a particular effort to keep his system free of religious connotations, so that it wouldn't be exclusive to followers of only one religion.

Over the past two decades, though, as soon as Reiki researchers went to Japan, they tended to be so fascinated by the serenity of the temples and monasteries that they added Buddhist teachings to Reiki. Having been to a number of seminars where the beautifully accessible Reiki was wrapped in rather inaccessible mystical teachings, I didn't want to fall into the same trap.

But maybe I was overthinking. After all, I was only going for the pictures…

Part II

Japan

14.

The Journey

A smile can make a big difference – I'm glad my journey started with a taxi driver's smile. Without it, I would have been even more miserable. Suffering from a bad cold, I was questioning the wisdom of a long-haul flight. Did I really need to go to Japan? Why not go somewhere nice and warm where I could relax on the beach? Changing flights in Munich, I had to buy lozenges for my sore throat.

The flight took 13 hours, and though I can normally sleep in the middle of Piccadilly Circus, I didn't sleep at all. Instead, I had a long and interesting conversation with the young man sitting next to me. He was a PhD student on his way to a conference in Tokyo about something to do with IT and therefore completely beyond my comprehension. His hobby, though, fascinated me: curating a Facebook page for the international community of a particular branch of the Coptic Church of North Africa, which dates back to the first century AD. I'd never heard of it before. We spoke about meaning, marriage, religious affiliations … and churches built in holes in the ground, which made sense when he showed me the pictures. He was excited by the Church's teachings and planned to live his life according to them.

In this surreal situation, somewhere above the clouds, racing over different continents and having a deep conversation with a stranger, my mind took a journey of its own. When my neighbour eventually drifted off to sleep, I pondered the question of religions...Were they really necessary? Why did so many people turn to them on their search for meaning? Why did we search for meaning at all? Was that the main reason for our existence on Earth? And did religions lead us in the right direction? How did Reiki fit in? Was it a religion, after all? Was it a religion for me?

No surprise that I couldn't sleep.

I thought back to my childhood, which had been remarkably religious. When I was about eight years old, I began going to church regularly, sometimes with my parents and most of the time with my grandmother. Over the years, I developed a deep interest in Christianity.

First of all I attended a relatively liberal Lutheran church, but in my early teens I was drawn to a more radical interpretation of Christianity and joined a denomination that was much stricter and more orthodox in its views. Looking back, I realise that I simply wanted clear answers. And I got them: 'You are in this world through God's grace, so live a decent life. If you are good, you'll go to heaven. If you aren't ... well ... you won't.'

This scared me. Interestingly, I was reasonably convinced that I would somehow manage to end up in heaven, but what about my friends? My classmates at school? Those family members who weren't very religious and who sometimes even gently mocked my extreme religiousness? Would they all end up in hell? I found that as difficult to accept as it was frightening, and certainly didn't want it to happen. I had to prevent it if possible. I must have been quite an annoying teenager, always trying to steer conversations to God, heaven and the deeper meaning of life, hoping that this might lead to a change in people's attitudes.

I was so convinced that people needed to believe in God and pray in order to avoid hell that, much to my parents' embarrassment, I ordered tons of leaflets from an evangelical organisation. They carried simple messages along the lines of 'Change now or end up in hell', complete with pretty graphic illustrations. I intended to walk along the beach during the summer holiday and hand them out to the sunseekers, but much to my parents' relief, they only arrived after the holiday. So one morning I stood at the school gate and handed them out to everybody.

Soon after I started, however, a teacher came up to me and told me that I wasn't allowed to distribute any marketing materials. Undaunted, I moved to just outside the school grounds, thinking to myself, 'This isn't marketing material – I'm trying to save people from hell!'

Watching the sunset from the plane, I had to smile at these early attempts to get people on what I thought was the right path. By then, of course, having received messages from people in the afterlife who weren't religious at all, it had become very clear to me that it wasn't as straightforward as I had been taught.

'If there *is* a hell,' I reflected, 'it's here on Earth.'

That may sound extreme, but what I had been through, not to mention what so many others had experienced in various shapes and forms, warranted, I felt, being classified as hell.

Really, hell is the temporary experience of feeling completely lost. Also, when we connect to what's beyond this world, everything is brighter, lighter and more positive. The energetic frequencies are higher. Hell is the experience of energetic density, of feeling lost, lonely, disconnected and singled out – and therefore by definition not part of the higher realms.

It took time, however, for me to realize that something in the Christian teachings (as I interpreted them) wasn't quite right. I even started studying theology at Hamburg University. It was when I applied a more academic approach that I started to ask questions, and then heaven and hell, sin and redemption somehow didn't fit into my world-view as snugly as they had before. Though I do realize today that Christianity is, as it were, a very broad Church and I was taking a narrow-minded sectarian view.

The final straw, though, was of a more personal nature. When I was in my early twenties, I became a member of my local church council. But I also fell in love. With a man.

I was convinced I had committed the greatest sin in the universe. I was certain to end up in hell.

And to my surprise, I didn't care. Even though it violated every belief I had ever held, it felt entirely right. I slowly accepted that I wasn't harming anyone, just experiencing romantic love, and my first boyfriend and I stayed together for almost three years.

Once I had accepted myself, I didn't want to hide from others, and decided to present him to the world: my family, the local conservative party, where I was chairman, and the church. To my surprise, the first two were remarkably accepting, and it turned out they'd had their suspicions anyway. But at church, the news didn't go down particularly well. I started to be ignored and even bullied on the council and was told I wasn't needed to give readings from the gospels on Sundays or hand out Holy Communion.

Before long, I had resigned from the council and moved away completely from that church. For years to come, my family laughed at me for taking a detour to work so that I wouldn't go past it. But I just couldn't bear being anywhere near it.

Years later, a book called *A Course in Miracles* did help to reconcile me with the core of Jesus' teachings, which didn't seem to differ much from the life lessons I'd learned by then. Today, I am surprised how often I quote Jesus on my courses.

However, I can wholeheartedly say that Reiki can work with any religious belief or none. It isn't about belief, but about experience.

With all these thoughts and memories whirling through my mind, I made my way through the skies to Japan...

15.

Lost in Japan

Despite my tiredness, once I got off the plane, I felt really excited. Something had shifted during those 13 hours of contemplating and it suddenly dawned on me that something significant might happen on this journey.

Even the energy around me felt different. I wondered whether this was because of my sudden nervousness. But later other people confirmed that there is a very strong 'spirit of place' in Japan, perhaps due to the intense volcanic activity.

As soon as I left the airport, though, more immediate concerns took over: to reach my hotel, I had to change trains several times – with two giant suitcases. The customs officer had already found them so suspicious that he had made me unpack them, only to find that they mainly contained boots and shoes for every potential change of weather. Much to my embarrassment.

Eventually I arrived at the hotel – and learned that they do things differently in Japan. The room was supposed to be ready at 2 p.m., but given that it was after noon, I was hoping it was already available.

'No problem at all,' said the friendly lady at reception. 'Your room is ready. You just need to pay an extra 50 dollars for early check-in.'

I politely declined, put my luggage into storage for a few hours (which was free of charge) and wondered why, as the room was empty anyway, I wasn't allowed to move in for free. It was only later that I learned about a business model apparently common in Japan: renting hotel rooms by the hour... Different countries, different customs. I was a long way from home.

Walking around Shinjuku, the local neighbourhood, what stood out to me was no matter how small the actual plots that the houses were built on, this didn't in any way determine their height. In European terms, many plots were tiny, almost of medieval size, probably once home to a small cottage or two-storey house. Now there were seven-storey high-rise buildings on them, the narrowest I had ever seen.

I walked around in wonder. There were illuminated signs on nearly every building, giving names and sometimes descriptions of what was on offer there – on the first, second and sometimes third floors too. I soon realised that shops and restaurants weren't confined to the ground floor. Tokyo was colourful, Tokyo was busy, Tokyo was loud. I can't say that I was particularly impressed. But maybe I was simply too tired.

And nervous. Even worried. Under pressure. After all, if this trip was meant to lead me to a deeper understanding, supposedly of something Reiki-related, I had to find it. How should I prepare? How open did I need to be? How vigilant?

Guidance is a strange thing... Sometimes it is patently obvious (but we still miss it), other times it's hard to recognise (and we surprise ourselves by spotting it the moment it appears). Now, would I see what I was meant to see? Or would my rational mind prevent me?

The first day put my mind at ease. Just down the road from my hotel I suddenly saw a billboard with one of the great loves of my life: a dog!

When I was a child, my dad didn't allow any pets. Especially dogs. They were dangerous, smelly and a lot of work. They would poo where they weren't supposed to. They were noisy as well – a particular problem for my dad.

I kind of adopted this take on dogs. But soon after I arrived in England, I met a new boyfriend. And a few weeks later, one evening I heard some strange noises on the wooden floor: he had brought his two mini Yorkshire terriers.

At first I thought they were utterly ridiculous and extremely embarrassing. I stayed a few steps behind him when we took them for a walk. But in less than a week I had been completely converted by their furry love.

When my partner and I split up around the time of the bankruptcy, he accepted that it would be best for all concerned if he left them with me and Mum, so they became our surprisingly understanding companions during that difficult time. They had a very keen sense of when we were struggling and would snuggle up to us on the sofa when we needed support. They often caused mayhem as well, but who cared? When they passed away several years later, we managed to live without a dog for less than a fortnight, then we went to a dogs' home and adopted the opposite of what we had before – a giant greyhound.

Today, if somebody wants to get my attention, they just need to walk their dog. I am guaranteed to stop and say hello!

In Shinjuku, even a picture did the trick. I looked right into the eyes of an incredibly beautiful dog, who, I later learned, was actually the most famous dog in Japan. For years, he had accompanied his owner to work and patiently waited outside. One day his owner didn't come out again, because he had died suddenly, but the dog waited outside the office every single day for the rest of his life.

Locals tried to adopt him. But he didn't want another home, another owner. So they fed him and just let him wait there. By the time he died, a few years later, he had become so well known that they built a memorial to him.

Unsurprisingly, a company then came up with the idea of using him to symbolise dedication and used his image as part of an advertising campaign. I have no idea what they were trying to sell, but there on the billboard, underneath the dog and the slogan, was a telephone number, and that was as clear a message as could be: 1111.

I had seen that number many times and in many places, and always when I felt lost. A few years earlier, for example, I had cleaned the fitted carpets in an apartment and subsequently they appeared to have shrunk. The estate agents held me liable and obtained a quote for replacing them, which I was nowhere near able to afford. But just after assessing the damage, I parked the car, put a few coins in the meter and, with a huge sigh of relief, saw that it would expire at 11.11 a.m. All would be well.

It subsequently turned out that the carpet had been over-stretched in the first place and the wet cleaning had just brought this to light. In the end, I didn't have to pay anything at all.

A bit more relaxed after seeing the billboard, I walked back to the hotel. By then, it was the pre-arranged check-in time and I went to my room and fell asleep straight away.

A couple of hours later, it was time to grab dinner – which was easier said than done. I found that in Japan a plastic version of almost every restaurant dish is displayed in the window. It shows you exactly what you get – if you are in the know. My problem was that I either wasn't quite sure what it was or it was something that I thought to be more of an acquired taste – like chicken ligaments, fermented fish, or algae.

Eventually, I found what looked like avocado on toast with salmon and egg on top. I thought I could probably handle that, but what actually arrived was avocado, raw, as expected, topped with salmon, also raw, which I hadn't thought of, and topped with an egg yolk, also … well, you get the idea.

I was quite hungry, and somehow survived. But I'd learned my lesson and over the next week ordered nothing but ramen noodles unless I was in the company of a Japanese guide.

16.

The Memorial Stone

When I woke up the next morning – lunchtime, to be precise – I headed straight for the one and only place I wanted to be sure of visiting in Tokyo: Mikao Usui's memorial stone, the only source of reliable information about his life.

Finding it was a bit of a challenge. For a start, the subway station where I was told to alight had several exits. Eventually I found the right one and ventured out, only to find myself on a shopping street. A few hundred yards along, I found a junction that looked like the one described on the internet, then looked out for a lamppost with the numbers indicating where to turn. And it wasn't there. I saw several lampposts, but none with numbers.

My mobile wasn't connected to a Japanese network, so Google Maps wasn't an option. Lost on my first day of Reiki research then – unless I switched to another source of directions.

I connected to Reiki and felt guided to take a little alleyway on my left. After a few minutes, there was a metal fence, and when I looked through it, I saw, to my great delight, tombstones: the graveyard of the Saihoji temple, home to Mikao Usui's grave and memorial stone!

A few hundred yards on, there was an entrance to a car park with a detailed map of the cemetery. It showed the locations of the family graves, and one had almost been wiped out by all the fingers that had pointed to it: the grave of the Usui family.

I meandered through the little walkways of the graveyard and finally saw a familiar shape through the trees: the memorial stone that I had seen in so many pictures. Now I would have my own picture of it.

The grave was slightly raised, with a lantern on the left, the memorial on the right and the tombstone in the centre. In front was a little altar, which was obviously much newer than the other features but made from a dark stone similar to that of the tomb. It had an opening for the burning of incense and was decorated with an engraving of the moon, the family crest of the Usuis.

I had definitely found it. What was I supposed to do now? I couldn't really have come all this way just to take pictures! But it was a good way to start, and I finally realised the reason why all the images I had seen showed the memorial at an angle: the frontal view is obscured by a large pine tree which throws shadows over the stone. I took pictures from every angle, including a selfie – my first ever – and one with my hand on it, pointing to the words *Rei* and *Ki*, which I had been able to decipher. The stone is about 10 feet tall and 4 feet wide, and the writing on it is rather small, so it contains quite a bit of information.

I took detailed pictures of every other item on the grave and walked up and down the neighbouring walkways to capture views of the memorial stone as part of the wider landscape.

My main job done, I sat down to meditate. At least I attempted to, because as soon as I closed my eyes, I heard the unmistakable sound of a mosquito.

Normally, this wouldn't have bothered me, but my tourist guidebook had informed me that a few years earlier Tokyo's parks had been closed during the summer months because of a sudden outbreak of dengue fever. Which, of course, is transmitted by mosquitoes.

That was it. No matter how hard I tried, I just couldn't relax. Certainly not concentrate. All that came into my mind was: 'Dengue fever, dengue fever, dengue fever.'

When the mosquito was joined by a wasp, I decided it was time to give up. Then I heard a voice.

'Disappointed?'

'Yes, I am, actually,' I thought. It was true, I was a bit disappointed. Not really with the place, but with myself. Or the universe. I had been hoping something would happen – something big, something important, something insightful. But what *had* happened? A mosquito had appeared. And a wasp.

'I don't want this to be a place of pilgrimage.'

There was that voice again. Where was it coming from? Was it my subconscious jumping in? Or my mind playing tricks on me?

'Reiki isn't about me, it's about the energy. Reiki isn't stronger in Japan. This isn't the only place it can be found. It can be found everywhere.'

Mikao Usui was speaking to me...?

17.

Mikao Usui

Reiki is not about Mikao Usui, as I had just been very clearly told. But he was its founder. So, who was he?

I had wondered about this ever since my very first Reiki course. The majority of the Reiki history we had been taught had covered his successors. The information given about his own life had seemed almost mythical: a man on a life-long exploration of spirituality was born a Buddhist and later turned to Christianity. He became a missionary and was one day asked by a pupil how Jesus could heal with his hands. Being unable to answer this, he embarked on a quest of finding out, and one day climbed a mountain where, after 21 days of meditation and fasting, he was given healing hands and the Reiki symbols appeared to him in heavenly spheres. Depending on the audience, other details were sometimes added, such as him taking a course in religious studies at an American university or working as a social worker and missionary in Japanese prisons. Students have been learning variations if this account ever since World War II.

It eventually became obvious that this story was created by Hawayo Takata, the first Reiki Master outside Japan, who was born to Japanese parents in Hawaii, and it was customized to appeal to an American audience in the 1950s and 60s.

Even when the Reiki world became aware of the existence of the memorial stone in the late 1990s, and further research in Japan brought forth additional information, many Reiki teachers stuck with the original version.

Hawayo Takata had learned Reiki in the mid-1930s from one of Usui's Master students, a gentleman called Chujiro Hayashi, who had just broken away from the Reiki Gakkai, the teaching organisation that Mikao Usui had founded. She can be credited with the amazing achievement of literally bringing Reiki to the entire world.

Strangely, it wasn't widely practised in Japan itself after the war, but some people continued to use it privately, and about 50 years later, Hayashi's teachings were revived by another student.

The story that had prevailed in Japan was that Usui had remained Buddhist throughout his life. He was said to have had a varied career, including stints as a journalist, a social worker in a prison and a Shinto missionary. (Shinto is the indigenous Japanese religion, traditionally headed by the Emperor.)

After a disruption in his career, he was said to have followed a path of deepening his spiritual understanding with the idea of reaching Anshin Ritsumei, a state of complete inner peace and acceptance that is said to be achieved by following rigorous disciplines. Eventually he spent three years in a Zen monastery in Kyoto, but as he hadn't reached Anshin Ritsumei, his abbot advised him to retreat to the mountains and follow a regime of fasting and meditation.

The rest of the story is similar to the traditional version: after 21 days, he suddenly saw light and felt a deeply spiritual energy that led to the discovery that he had healing hands.

This version is factually more correct and also corroborated by the few students speaking outside the confines of the Reiki Gakkai, which today is run like a secret lodge, with new members having to be recommended by two existing ones. It has also been reportedly confirmed by one of its ex-presidents.

Interestingly, though, at least to a certain degree, neither account is correct. The true story of Mikao Usui is extraordinary, and I suppose it is time to relate it here, as much of it is on the memorial stone. I will give additional information, too, and will later make clear how I obtained this.

It still puzzles me just how little of the key information on the memorial stone has really been shared. Was this deliberate? Maybe an attempt by established Reiki teachers to avoid questioning the accuracy of what they were teaching?

Anyway, this is the original story of Reiki as I came to understand it.

Mikao Usui was born on 15 August 1865 in the small village of Taniai in the Gifu district of Japan, a rather remote and slightly rugged area with small mountains and deep valleys. He had two brothers and a sister, and the family ran a local retail and wholesale business, which was continued by the sister. When I visited it in 2016, the village store was still run by the wife of her grandson.

Apparently, they were comparatively well-off, and the names of Mikao Usui and his brothers can be found on the sides of a *torii* – a gate which they donated to the local shrine.

It seems that half of the village carries the surname of Usui – at least seven or eight large families, even though they aren't related. The memorial stone mentions that this goes back to Chiba Tsunetane, a famous Samurai warrior who, in the 12th century, captured the city of Usui. Subsequently, all his soldiers were allowed to use this name as their surname. Indeed, up to the mid-19th century, only the Samurai were allowed to carry surnames at all.

When Mikao Usui was born, though, the privileges of the Samurai were about to be abolished. He would not have worn the traditional top-knot hairstyle or been granted an automatic right to a position in the civil service, police or army.

Today, Taniai could easily be described as a rather boring place, and I assume it wouldn't have been very different in Usui's time. My guidebook listed a thousand-year-old cherry tree as the main attraction of the greater area. When I visited, I learned that about a third of the population had moved away since the 1950s, a trend that had apparently already started in Mikao Usui's time. He and his younger brother moved to Tokyo when they were in their late teens. At least Taniai does have a school today; in the 19th century, the education of young children was in the hands of the local monastery. The first education Mikao Usui would therefore have received would have been in a Buddhist temple in the Pure Land tradition. He would later have visited a school in a nearby town.

The memorial stone says he 'surpassed his fellows in hard work and endeavour', and the Usui brothers left their village with great aspirations. Tokyo, the thriving commercial and administrative centre of Japan, would be full of opportunities. While his brother studied to become a medical doctor, Mikao Usui seems to have been rather undecided and tried out several different careers. But the memorial stone mentions that his will to succeed was one of his main characteristics.

He would certainly have seized any opportunities to meet influential people, and eventually gained employment as the personal assistant of a well-known politician, Shinpei Goto. Eight years older than Mikao Usui and also from a Samurai family, he was already well established by the time they met. And although Usui's actual job was a low-level one, it would have allowed him to be at the side of a remarkable person.

Even a short summary of his career is awe-inspiring:

Born in 1857, he trained as a medical doctor, then became president of the Nagoya Medical School at the age of 25 and subsequently head of the Home Ministry's medical department, publishing his principles of national health in 1890.

He later advised the Japanese government of Taiwan and became the island's first civilian governor in 1898, then took over of the enormous infrastructure project of the South Manchuria Railway Company.

He served in a number of Japanese administrations as minister, with portfolios ranging from Railways and Communication to the Home Office in 1916 and Foreign Office in 1918.

In 1920, he became mayor of Tokyo city, and he led the rebuilding of the city after the earthquake in 1923 – a job he continued when he returned to the position of home secretary in 1924.

During this time, he was presented with a prototype of a pocket watch by a Japanese company. Realising the potential of the product, he decided to name it Citizen and expressed his hope that one day such a luxury item would become available to ordinary citizens. Subsequently, the company renamed itself Citizen and became a brand that is still recognized worldwide.

In all his positions, Shinpei Goto left a lasting legacy as a modernizer and reformer, and in later years was also engaged in establishing the scouting movement in Japan, becoming the country's first Chief Scout.

The more I read about this man, the more impressed I was. I am sure it would have been the same for Mikao Usui, who eventually crossed paths with Goto again in the 1920s. Interestingly, though, Usui first went in a very different direction – you could say he took a detour. Having inherited a strong entrepreneurial spirit, he started to build his own business.

By the age of 30, he had made it: he had a thriving import and export business, moved in the highest social circles and made cutting-edge deals. He would borrow huge sums and invest them in complete shipments of goods from overseas, betting on the fact that once they arrived in Japan, he would be able to sell them at a huge mark-up. It was remarkably successful.

He didn't specialise, but imported anything he assumed would be popular, including household goods, machinery and even fashionable clothes to fulfil the demand generated by a more westernized taste in Japanese society. He often travelled on the ships himself and was able to broaden his perspective by visiting Europe and the USA, at the same time identifying new trends and products.

In his social life, he was just as active. He liked attending parties and dinners and meeting interesting people, and with his good looks and charming personality, he was a welcome guest, particularly when it came to the ladies. He enjoyed the attention, and it would be fair to say that he was a bit of a ladies' man.

Witty, sharp and well versed in everything from history to culture and the Japanese arts, he knew how to entertain people and loved life. But there was already a deeper, more spiritual side to him.

He had a huge interest in the Japanese and Chinese spiritual traditions, sometimes even bordering on the nationalistic, as he was a great admirer of the Japanese Emperor. He would spend a great deal of his time studying, with the aim of advancing as a person and gaining a deeper spiritual understanding of the world. He had the strong sense that there were secrets in the universe that could be uncovered.

You could say there were two, sometimes conflicting, aspects to his personality: the successful man of the world and the spiritual seeker. Even as a young man, before he embarked on his entrepreneurial career, he studied in China, as the memorial stone reveals.

He also engaged in martial arts as part of his personal development and was fascinated by the abilities that generations of Samurai were reported to have had: palm healing and an understanding of moon cycles, astrology and auspicious signs, as well as a tradition of civic-mindedness and protecting their families and friends.

He found that many of these traditional values still prevailed in the military, and formed many close connections and friendships with like-minded officers. Over time, friends would not just see him as a successful businessman, but also as a remarkable teacher of esoteric disciplines, who drew his knowledge from Buddhist, Shinto and Taoist traditions.

Then, sometime after his 50th birthday, things started to go pear-shaped. The memorial stone mentions that 'in the face of adversity, he strove to train himself even more with the courage never to yield'. (I am using the translation by my friend Hyakuten Inamoto, a Buddhist monk who is well-versed in Japanese history and spiritual traditions.) He tried to make things work, making riskier and riskier deals in the hope that the next one would be the turning-point. But his luck had deserted him. In the end, he went bankrupt.

The term, however, is not entirely correct, as Japan only introduced a bankruptcy law a few years later. This meant that he was in no way safeguarded. Due to his huge debts, he lost his business, his money, his house and his ability to support his family. Not to mention his social position. Suddenly he was persona non grata. And, even worse, so were his wife and children.

As the memorial stone states, Mikao Usui 'fell into great difficulties'.

For me, this is the most important sentence on the entire memorial. And strangely, the most overlooked. It is as if Reiki teachers don't want to admit that there was a time when the founder failed in life!

The importance of the wording on the stone becomes even more evident when we look at who composed the text: Juzaburo Ushida, one of Usui's Master students, his successor as president of the Reiki Gakkai and a vice-admiral of the Japanese navy – a person whose reputation would be called into question if he were seen to be associating with the 'wrong kind of people'. And who had set out to make sure that Mikao Usui would be remembered as a revered teacher for generations to come.

This is all the more significant in that it is simply is not part of Japanese culture to mention something like a business failure. So Usui's would not have appeared on the memorial stone unless he himself had spoken of it. It is clear that he didn't want to present himself as a saint. He wanted his system to be open to everyone and to reach people who had also gone through difficulties.

It is truly remarkable that this information has been kept under wraps for most of the 20th century.

The mention of Usui's 'difficulties' on the memorial stone also highlights a key element of life: difficulties change us. Voluntarily or involuntarily, we cannot continue with life as before. And this is an amazing opportunity!

When I ask why people want to learn Reiki, the vast majority refer to going through difficult times.

And of course, without my own bankruptcy, I would probably have had no need to embark on a more spiritual path.

Having failed to get back on his feet, Mikao Usui could have taken an option that is very much part of Japanese culture: suicide.

To this day, Japan has the highest number of suicides in the 'developed' world. And the cultural attitude towards it is unique: it is seen as a way of accepting responsibility rather than backing out, an honourable way of restoring the family's reputation.

But Mikao Usui's many years of spiritual development led him in another direction: he concluded that the universe wanted him to change his path. With his family being looked after by his brother the wealthy doctor, he moved to Kyoto and joined a monastery. Maybe there he would find a way forward.

Interestingly, he didn't.

And this is what so many Reiki researchers miss: the way to a deeper understanding of Reiki doesn't lie in retreating to a Buddhist monastery or delving into ancient religious scriptures. It lies in applying it in real life.

Even in the monastery, Mikao Usui's difficulties continued. For the next three years he tried to follow every spiritual exercise in the textbook: meditation and fasting; silence and mindfulness; chanting and drumming; community work and gardening; reading, debating and contemplating. None of it worked for him, or at least not to the degree he'd hoped for. None led to the meaningful change he was longing for...

Every avenue he'd taken had turned into a dead end. It seemed there was nowhere else to go.

Except *away*. Mikao Usui left Kyoto and began to walk away, faster and faster, as if he had to leave the whole world behind. But he did have a destination in mind.

Several hours later, he reached it: Mount Kurama, a place he'd been to many times before.

Situated north of Kyoto, the mountain had been home to Buddhist temples for over a thousand years and a large area of its western flank had been filled with temples and shrines. In the early 20th century, the complex belonged to the Buddhist Tendai tradition and was overseen by a temple in Kyoto.

Usui's destination wasn't a temple, though, or a bed in a monastery. He went beyond the temples and shrines to the top of the mountain. And stayed there.

He did what he had never done before: he surrendered.

He would fast and meditate ... and leave it to the universe to sort things out. And if that meant he would stay on that mountain for the rest of his life, so what? There was no other option left.

He didn't just surrender to the universe, but also to nature during a very cold March. Many nights the temperature dipped below zero and there was a very real risk of freezing to death. He did have a few blankets and covers, provided by some monks from the Kurama temple who knew that he was there, and he could also use a basic shelter meant for meditation. But often he had to use the breathing and willpower techniques that he had learned in the martial arts and Samurai traditions to focus his energy at night, and sometimes he just had to keep moving till dawn. Many nights, he didn't sleep at all.

He had been living in a big city ever since his teens and this kind of life didn't feel normal to him. But he accepted it. To his surprise, he slowly began to see the animals around him as company, and even began to establish a level of communication with them. But he would never ask his future students to go through anything remotely similar, although he did joke about it.

Even though he accepted the risk of dying, he wasn't seeking death. There were times when he was deeply scared. Of the wild animals, the cold, the future. He wasn't always able to stay in surrender mode either. Many a time he was about to give up and simply walk back.

The problem was, there was no back. He couldn't go back to the monastery – they wouldn't have accepted him again. And he couldn't go back to his family – that wouldn't have been socially acceptable.

But the times of despair were interspersed with moments of hope, sometimes hours of hope. They were almost blissful states in which he found total peace and wished he could stay that way forever.

But of course sometimes he recalled the events that had led him to the mountain. He recalled the successes, the fun times, the beautiful experiences. But he also recalled the nightmares, the sleepless nights, the experience of losing everything. All these memories had one thing in common: they were what they were. The past couldn't be changed. There was no point in holding on to it. It was just part of the strange concept of time, part of the fleetingness of life.

18.

Light

Mikao Usui stayed on the mountain for three weeks. Then he saw light. Literally. He saw nothing but light, a brightness that was almost blinding.

Initially, it felt as if the light was shining down from above, as if the whole forest was floodlit. But it didn't stop there. Mikao Usui could *feel* the light too, as if it was going through his body. He felt it as love. As everything that could be desired. And more.

Something had opened up – a door, a gateway, a connection. And his chakras.

He had experienced the original Reiki attunement.

Every subsequent attunement is designed to recreate that experience and result, even though at the time Usui wasn't even aware of the effect it would have.

He later described it as feeling a 'big Reiki' above his head. That was the first time that the word *Reiki* was used in connection with the system he later developed. The feeling of pressure or pulling on the top of the head is a common experience in today's Reiki attunements and it means that the crown chakra is opening. Once I made this connection, I finally started to realise that my experience of seeing the colour purple in my Reiki 1 attunement was really a repetition of Usui's experience.

The word *Reiki* would have been commonly understood in his time. It is part of a world-view that distinguishes between seven energetic levels in the universe, a bit like the layers of the human aura. The highest, lightest, all-encompassing one was called *Rei-Ki* – the energy that connects the universe to its Source, the creative force behind its existence, the beginning and the end. Eternity. God.

Mikao Usui later described his system as being *based on* Reiki, though he never called the system itself by that name.

But he had obtained the experiential knowledge that beyond darkness, sadness and separation, there is light. Negativity, fear, even outright horror and despair are only ever temporary. Light is eternal. He had seen that: he had experienced *enlightenment*. The Japanese word for that is *satori*: a moment of sudden understanding, of seeing the world as it is.

On the memorial stone, all this is summed up in the very simple words: 'One day, he climbed Kurama-yama [Mt Kurama] and after 21 days of severe discipline without eating, he suddenly felt One Great Reiki over his head and attained enlightenment and he obtained Reiki Ryoho.'

Reiki Ryoho is the Reiki *method*. Usui wasn't aware of this yet. But he did know that he had reached the level of spiritual connection that he had dreamed of all his life. The change he had undergone was so profound that he knew he could go back to his family and be seen as having made up for his difficult past.

As he got back on his feet and started to move around, slowly and slightly uneasily, he caught his big toe on a semi-exposed root, tearing off the nail.

What an interesting challenge: he just had the most incredible spiritual experience of his life and his very next step had led to an injury. He could still feel the light inside, the deep spiritual connection, but he was also in his human body, and that body was hurting rather badly.

In the absence of any medical help or supplies, he cleaned the wound with icy water and intuitively placed his hands around it. This is termed *teate*, palm healing, and is still well known in Japan. One of my Japanese students told me that when she was young, whenever she accidentally hurt herself her parents would place their hands around the wound with the intention of supporting the healing. But they would mainly expect to see psychological effects rather than physical results.

With Mikao Usui, though, the results were very different: the bleeding stopped almost straight away, the pain receded and he witnessed the onset of healing. He was completely overwhelmed and immediately realised what this meant: his experience of enlightenment had opened up a channel to high-vibrational energy that could be used for healing. He had seen the light and was now able to administer 'light healing'.

He tore a strip from his kimono, bandaged his toe to shield it and began his walk back to normality. Contrary to popular belief, he didn't walk down the back of the mountain, which would have seen him end up in the hamlet of Kibune, but decided to take the route past the temples, so that he could stop and thank the universe.

He didn't want anyone to see him, so he sneaked into the main temple and knelt down in a dark corner, wondering whether anybody would spot the light that he still felt inside. Nobody came in, and he remained there for a long time in gratitude and bliss.

On his way back to Kyoto, an often-related event occurred: when he asked for a glass of water, the girl who brought it to him was in obvious distress. Her swollen jaw indicated a badly inflamed tooth and she was in great pain. An opportunity to put his healing hands to work!

After asking permission from her father, Mikao Usui placed his hands on her jaw. And lo and behold, the swelling went down, the pain subsided and she started to feel much better.

Just to reiterate the point that is probably obvious already, Mikao Usui didn't set out to find a complementary healing system. It was a by-product of a spiritual experience. The author of the memorial stone mentions this several times: '[He] newly founded the method based on the Reiki of the universe.'

Strangely, this hasn't stopped a huge number of Reiki teachers telling their students that Mikao Usui rediscovered a healing system in ancient scriptures…

He first tried healing family and friends. And, as the memorial stone says, it worked immediately. He had no doubt that this wasn't just a temporary phenomenon, but here to stay. He also had no doubt that because the energy was flowing from such a high level, Reiki, the seventh level of the universe, he was using pure light – Source energy.

With his confidence firmly established, everything moved very quickly. It was as if his entrepreneurial qualities had reappeared, to be put to use in a very different context. Within a few weeks, he had found a small place in Harajuku, Tokyo, where he could live with his family and give Reiki treatments.

More and more he discovered that there wasn't really much he needed to do apart from being aware of his hands, where they wanted to be placed, the energy flowing through his body and the guidance coming to him. He soon developed a sense of what was going on with a client and where Reiki was needed.

He had become a tool of the light and just needed to trust that it knew what to do.

More and more people began to seek his help, amazed by the fact that his technique was so easy and effective. Nobody had to believe in anything, and Usui loved to surprise his clients with an amazing transformation.

He could easily have styled himself as a unique and enlightened super-healer. But he felt this would be egotistical. It would mean assuming he was the only person who could do such a thing. And that wasn't his belief. He was convinced that everybody was connected to the very same Source and could access the same healing power.

But how could that work? How could people make the connection that was constantly open to him? He started to experiment, again first with family and friends.

Interestingly, it didn't even occur to him to send people into the wilderness, to have them leave their families and potentially risk their lives to go through what he had on Mt Kurama. That had been the path for him, but it wouldn't be for others.

At this point, his decades of trying out different esoteric traditions kicked in. Some used powerful initiation rituals that allowed a master to open up the energetic abilities of the students or connect them with particular meditation tools. In some yoga traditions, for instance, attunements are used even today. They are normally performed by an Acharya, a senior swami or yogic master, and are designed to connect a student with a personal mantra, so they can use this as a gateway to higher vibrations and spiritual development.

In a way, Mikao Usui needed to create an opening for his students that was as powerful as the one he had had when he saw the light on Mt Kurama. He therefore developed a method of strongly focusing on this light himself and then establishing a connection with his student so that they could sense the very same gateway – *attune* themselves to it, as it were. The Japanese word for 'attunement' is *Reiju*, which can roughly be translated as 'energy blessing'.

To his great excitement, it worked: his students started to develop the abilities that he had. They could use Reiki for themselves and they could give Reiki treatments to others. He had taken the first steps towards what today we call the system of Reiki.

Over the next few months, though, Usui began to realise that there were differences between his students. Some were very intuitive and open; others took a significant amount of time to be aware of and accept their new abilities.

He developed his teachings accordingly, and gradually introduced the three Reiki symbols. He also established different levels of teaching, starting with *Shoden* (Reiki 1, the 'beginner's teachings'), then *Okuden* (Reiki 2, the 'inner teachings'), and eventually, a few years later, *Shinpiden* (the Master/teacher level, the 'mystery teachings').

His great breakthrough came a year later.

On Saturday 1st September 1923, the ground in Tokyo started to shake. Even for an earthquake-prone country, this was a big one. Measuring 7.9 on the Richter scale, and with its epicentre close to Tokyo, it became the worst natural disaster in Japanese history. Named after the Kanto Plain that Tokyo is built on, the Great Kanto Earthquake destroyed large swathes of the city. To make matters worse, it happened around lunchtime, when many people were cooking over open fires, causing fires that raged for days amid almost apocalyptic scenes. Estimates of fatalities range from 140,000 to 170,000 people.

The memorial stone mentions this turning-point:

> *In September of the 12th year (AD 1923) there was a great earthquake and a conflagration broke out. Everywhere there were groans of pain from the wounded. [Mikao Usui], feeling pity for them, went out every morning to go around the town, and he cured and saved an innumerable number of people. This is just a broad outline of his relief activities during such an emergency.*

He was often accompanied by students and as a result became well known not just in Tokyo, but throughout Japan. Even his old friend and mentor Shinpei Goto, at that time mayor of the city, took care to acknowledge his help.

Soon his house in Harajuku couldn't accommodate the growing number of students and clients and he built a bigger one further out of town.

He began to turn his method into a complete system, giving guidelines for hand positions, breathing and energy-cleansing techniques and meditation, all designed to strengthen the energetic connection and to help students to trust their intuition and let go of their ego.

Particularly important, though, were two elements that he added at this time: *Gokai* and *Gyosei*, principles and poems.

The author of the memorial stone makes very clear how central they were and how they helped to shift his own understanding of Reiki from a complementary therapy to a path of self-development:

> *On reflection,* Reiho *[Reiki method] puts special emphasis not just on curing diseases, but also on enjoying well-being in life with correcting the mind and making the body healthy with the use of an innate healing ability. Thus, before teaching, the* Ikun *[admonition] of the Meiji Emperor should reverently be read and Five Precepts be chanted and kept in mind mornings and evenings.*
>
> *First it reads, 'Today do not be angry,' secondly it reads, 'Do not worry,' thirdly it reads, 'Be thankful,' fourthly it reads, 'Work with diligence,' fifthly it reads, 'Be kind to others.'*

These are truly great teachings for cultivation and discipline that agree with the great teachings of the ancient sages and the wise. [Mikao Usui] named these teachings 'Secret Method to Invite Happiness and 'Miraculous Medicine to Cure All Disease'; notice the outstanding features of the teachings. Furthermore, when it comes to teaching, it should be as easy and common as possible, nothing lofty. Another noted feature is that during sitting in silent meditation with [the hand position] Gassho *and reciting the Five Precepts mornings and evenings, the pure and healthy mind can be cultivated and put into practice in one's daily routine. This is the reason why* Reiho *is easily obtained by anyone.*

Recently the course of the world has shifted and a great change in thought has taken place. Fortunately, with the spread of this [spiritual method], there will be many that supplement the way of the world and the minds of people. How can it be for just the benefit of curing chronic diseases and longstanding complaints?

The Reiki precepts, or principles, were designed as a way of bringing the spiritual awareness gained from Reiki into everyday life.

Usui also gave his students a booklet with 125 poems written by the Meiju Emperor as a tool for reflection and inspiration, which, as we will see in a moment, can have a huge impact even today.

The system that Mikao Usui created only developed under his guidance for four years. While travelling and teaching outside Tokyo, he unexpectedly died from a stroke on 9th March 1926.

And now I was standing at the grave of this incredible man.

'Disappointed?'

I could almost hear an echo of that voice. But how ridiculous! How could I possibly be disappointed? At a historical place connected with such a man! And almost seeming to hear him speaking to me...

But yes, in a way I was disappointed. After all, I knew most of the information on the memorial stone already. And the bits that were missing I only learned much later.

Yes, Mikao Usui was amazing. Superlative. No question about it. After all, that was why I learned Reiki in the first place. It was right to honour him. But did I have to come all this way for that? Or was it really just for the pictures? I still didn't know.

19.

A Word from the Emperor

The next morning I got up early for a change, as I was due to leave for Kyoto in the afternoon, and went to Harajuku, the neighbourhood where Mikao Usui had established his first treatment and teaching centre. Today, it is the epicentre of Japanese street fashion and filled with teenagers in the most astonishing outfits, but somehow it still manages to retain the feel of Tokyo 100 years ago. There are no high-rise buildings and instead the many alleyways, too small for modern cars, are lined with one- and two-storey houses. Walking down one of the streets, I suddenly had the strong feeling I was very near where the Usui family had lived.

Interestingly, the centre of Harajuku is just a few minutes' walk away from a historically important site, the Meiji-Jingu. Situated in a huge inner-city forest, this giant shrine was built for the Meiji Emperor and his wife. It is well known how much Mikao Usui admired him – the booklet with 125 of the Emperor's poems, written in the short waka style, that he gave to his students is testimony to that. Was proximity to the shrine the reason for his choice of residence?

It certainly would have given him some kind of anchor to be near the grave of such a person. After all, Emperor Mutsohito, posthumously named Emperor Meiji (1852–1912), can not only be credited with transitioning Japan from centuries of isolation and feudalism to a modern, democratic, and industrialized superpower, but also with introducing major reforms in education and healthcare and laying out moral principles for society.

One way of introducing his guidance to the public was through tens of thousands of waka poems for reflection.

Many Shinto temples offer a divination box for visitors. For a small fee, you shake it until a stick appears through a little hole. The number it bears corresponds to a message that is given to you by a warden and meant to help with current questions or decisions. The same is on offer at the Meiji Shrine, only here you are given a waka poem from the Emperor's *oeuvre*. Mine read:

> *If we falter in resolve*
> *just because the task is hard,*
> *no accomplishment can follow:*
> *it is the world's way.*

This wasn't quite what I had expected. What was going on? I'd thought my difficulties were behind me. Was there a new challenge to come on my trip?

Feeling even more nervous, I made my way back to the hotel. At least I tried to. I knew I had to change subways at some stage, but when I looked at the map, I got completely lost: the usual English translations of the names of the stations were missing and I didn't have a clue how to get home. I'd never felt so foreign in my life, but in the end I saw the funny side of it and somehow managed to catch the right train.

I collected my suitcases and took the Shinkansen, Japan's famous bullet train, to Kyoto.

Kyoto's train station was the most confusing I had ever encountered – a futuristic arched glass-and-steel building that looked more like a shopping centre. A few days later I did find an amazing kimono for Mum in the department store it houses, but initially I was more concerned with finding the right exit.

Mission finally accomplished, I dragged my luggage along a busy highway and passed a very long temple wall. Peering through the gates, I could see that the beauty and intricacy of the temple building were stunning.

My guidebook informed me that there were no fewer than 1,700 Buddhist temples in Kyoto, plus 800 Shinto shrines, and it was often referred to as the spiritual capital of Japan. No wonder that Mikao Usui picked this city as the place to deepen his spiritual understanding.

I arrived at my hotel, dumped my luggage and ventured out to find a place to eat. I didn't fancy another raw egg yolk and even contemplated visiting a well-known American fast-food chain (I honestly did!), but then found that there was a local Irish pub which might have something edible to offer. Indeed it did – I've rarely enjoyed a meal as much as that vegetable bake.

The pub was mainly frequented by expats, but that evening there was also a group of Japanese students there, looking to brush up their English. We started chatting, but my attempts to explain what I did for a living weren't entirely successful. I was either mispronouncing the word *Reiki* or they had simply never heard of it. In the end, I just drew the Japanese symbols for *Rei* and *Ki*. That got their attention: they were shocked! Did I work with ghosts? Apparently this is how young Japanese interpret the combination of the words for 'spirit' and 'energy' today. I had to reassure them that I was perfectly normal.

The system of Reiki is indeed very little known in Japan. It almost died out after World War II and has only recently been reintroduced. Was it perhaps necessary to pluck it out of Japan in order to take it to the rest of the world?

I am almost inclined to see it this way, as the language barrier is just too high to allow Japanese concepts to be easily disseminated on an international level. I heard the Dalai Lama once say that when he visited Japan, he always reminded people to learn English, otherwise they would never be able to properly engage with the rest of the world.

20.

The Real Kurama

The next day, I couldn't wait to get out of bed. After all, I was finally near Mt Kurama, the place where Mikao Usui had achieved enlightenment.

I took a train to the outskirts of Kyoto, then a tiny two-carriage train with Kurama as its final destination. Unbeknownst to me, millions of Japanese children had already taken this train, albeit not in a physical capacity. There is a famous computer game for children in which they can drive the train up into the mountains. In real life, the journey takes about 20 minutes and meanders higher and higher. Most of the mountains are covered by forests, but in between there are beautiful open vistas. No wonder that this line, the Keihan Railway, was built, in the late 1920s, not just to serve the local community but also to carry tourists.

Yet, as pretty as it was, it didn't quite meet my expectations. These weren't the Himalayas. Not even the Alps or the Rocky Mountains. Personally, I would be inclined to call them hills rather than mountains. Perhaps I'm just difficult to please.

Kurama railway station was a tiny but pretty place with ornate wood carvings – and a vendor selling freshly baked croissants to the tourists. The car park in front was overlooked by a large bright red hobgoblin with a very long nose. Was this an outpost of Disneyland?

Being offered a range of souvenirs featuring the hobgoblin, I subsequently discovered that it was meant to be a sculpture of the 'mountain spirit'. It didn't look particularly friendly, and afterwards I found it to be a pretty accurate depiction of the strange, not very pleasant, almost frightening energy that can be felt on the top of the mountain. This energy would have been an additional challenge for Mikao Usui.

Walking out of the station car park, I turned left into Kurama's high street, which was a bit of an exaggeration, as it only consisted of about seven or eight shops and tea rooms. Then I saw the colossal entrance to the Kurama Dera temple complex.

An impressive set of stone steps, flanked by orange lanterns, led to a large orange gate. I paid a small admission fee and entered, well, a Buddhist theme park – temples, shrines and gates, large and small, all very pretty and all very well kept. The stone steps were flanked by even more lanterns, and reasonably fit visitors could walk to the peak in 30 or 40 minutes. Others could take a cable car.

It was pretty. Scenic. But a place to face death? To achieve enlightenment?

As I slowly walked up the steps, past a little waterfall, curved wooden bridges and numerous shrines, some of which were selling protective and empowering amulets, I found myself getting annoyed. I hadn't come here to buy – literally – into superstition. I was looking for truth. For clarity. Was I in the wrong place?

The huge number of visitors didn't enhance the spiritual atmosphere either. One couple had dressed their tiny chihuahua up in a pink coat and were making her pose between the legs of a lion statue in front of a temple. Later I found out that I had visited on a bank holiday, and that popular tourist guidebooks described Kurama as perfect for a day out of Kyoto.

Admittedly, the scenery was beautiful, with giant trees, some of which were on the UN natural world heritage list, the lovely old stone steps (rather a lot of them) and the ubiquitous orange lanterns showing the way.

Three-quarters of the way up, I finally reached the impressive forecourt of the main temple. Inside, a ceremony was taking place with monks drumming and chanting – two monks, I later discovered, though it sounded like more. Next to the temple you could buy candles, fans and lucky charms (no further comment).

Escaping the crowds, I sat down in a little shrine and tried to meditate again. After 30 seconds, a mosquito arrived, buzzing right next to my ear. What was it about mosquitoes and meditation? I politely waved it away. Then I started to wonder about the difference between us. Was there any? Was there any ranking? I could have killed it, but didn't. I knew that one day I would be killed myself, or, I hoped, die of natural causes. Would we both return to spirit when we died? Were we connected to the same source? Had I needed to travel to Japan to meet an oriental mosquito? Weren't there mosquitoes in London too?

It was clearly time to move on. Too much orange for one day. The sun was about to set and I made my way down the mountain.

Time to relax. The village of Kurama hosts one of the few natural hot springs near Kyoto and I watched the sun setting behind Mount Kurama from the comfortable confines of a warm pool.

Happily soaking away, I had no idea that just a few months later, another *onsen* would be backdrop to a miraculous encounter.

I did have one special experience on Mt Kurama, though. Even now, I consider it one of the deepest spiritual experiences of my life. It involved a sculpture and a rope.

About halfway up the mountain there was a two-storey temple. The ground floor was a tea room selling green tea-flavoured ice cream, the upper floor the actual temple. The entrance was fairly hidden and most people just walked past. But I gave the ice cream a miss and went in.

At the front of the temple there was a roofed fountain. Familiar with the customary preparation for entering a temple, thanks to my guidebook, I picked up the ladle provided with my right hand, rinsed my left, then moved the ladle to my left hand to rinse my right and finally poured some water into my left hand and took a sip to rinse my mouth. This is the ritual on which *Kenyoku-Ho*, the energy-cleansing exercise in Reiki, seems to be based. Then I entered the main hall.

A giant statue of the Amida Buddha, the Amida Nyorai, dominated the room from the far side and I walked towards the bridge that divided the temple in two in order to get a better look at it. Its eyes were looking down, and when I followed them, I noticed that there were a few steps to a lowered area underneath the bridge. I went there and knelt down – the only way to fit in – and suddenly found myself right in front of the statue and looking straight into the Buddha's eyes. I wasn't in Disneyland anymore. There was something very real about it. The eyes were asking, 'Why are you here? What are you seeking?'

I was puzzled. Then I noticed something I hadn't seen before: a rope with one end tied to one of the hands of the statue and the other end lying in front of me, inviting me to pick it up and make a connection. To a statue?

Hesitatingly, I gave it a try. Of course, I knew it was a symbolic gesture, just as statues themselves are symbolic.

It's difficult to describe what happened next. I felt a very profound connection indeed. But to what?

Then I heard a voice, and it was very, very clear: 'Don't look here for enlightenment! It is within you. Everything is within.' And again: 'It is within. Look within. *Stop* searching outside yourself.'

It couldn't have been more direct. I was being told … off. And it felt amazing.

The Amida Nyorai and its Sanskrit symbol, *hrih*, are the inspiration behind one of the Reiki symbols, which in the West is called the Harmony Symbol. And its function is exactly the same: to make a connection to universal guidance.

As I held the rope, I knew I had made that connection.

21.

Temples, Mountains, and an American Lady

Over the next few days I saw the sights, as any tourist would. And, uncomfortably, I actually felt like one. I was still wondering whether there was a deeper meaning to my journey. Since the encounter with the statue of Amida Nyorai I had been feeling a bit more at ease, but was that really it?

After spending one Saturday morning with c.100,000 other tourists at Fushimi Inari-Taisha, a Shinto shrine sprawling up an entire mountain dedicated to the gods of rice and sake, I just wanted to escape.

Fortunately, I had a guide for the rest of the weekend, Michi, who had volunteered to show me the less touristy spots. I had never met him before, but it seems the universe had put us in touch. He had visited a mutual friend in Germany a month earlier, around the time I'd been asking for some advice about Japan. My friend had passed my question on to him and he'd offered to show me around. I have no idea how I would have managed without him. That first day he showed me a number of both obvious and hidden sights in the old district of Gion, then took me for dinner in a little restaurant only frequented by locals. Walking through the famous nightlife district afterwards, we even saw a Geisha! (Well, a trainee, but better than nothing.)

On Sunday, Michi picked me up from my hotel at 9 a.m. He had arranged for us to take part in an English language Zazen. *Zazen* means 'just sitting' and is the basic Zen meditation practice. The head priest led us through the ceremony and gave a fabulous account of the scientifically proven benefits of meditation, followed by a tour of the 16th-century monastery and some Matcha tea and sweets.

The 20-minute breathing exercise was simple and very effective: breathe in ... breathe out, making your exhalation twice as long. It's a fantastic way of releasing stress and clearing energetic blockages.

After this exercise, I decided to check out if Reiki felt different – and it did. It felt deeper. The emptier the vessel, I suppose, the more it can be filled with Reiki... I now start many of my Reiki workshops with this breathing exercise.

The temple had beautifully decorated sliding doors, which reminded me how important the choice of home décor was. I wondered about getting rid of some of the 'challenging' pictures by semi-psychopathic artists that I had bought when I was in my twenties...

And I learned that green tea should be served at 65–85 degrees, otherwise it tastes bitter. Finally, an explanation of why I'd never liked green tea! (To be honest, I'm still not a real fan, but it has its benefits for meditation and concentration.)

In the afternoon, we went to Mt Hiei, one of the most famous spiritual sites in Japan. The birthplace of Tendai Buddhism in the eighth century, for centuries it was a monastic powerhouse, with over 3,000 buildings in its heyday. Today over 120 temples remain. Given that Mikao Usui followed Tendai Buddhism, he would surely have been there too.

Mt Hiei was one of the most beautiful and spiritual places I had ever visited – even the busloads of tourists faded into the background. There was definitely something very special about Japan, and I was feeling more and more deeply connected to it.

My guidebook, though, reminded me of the stranger side of the mountain: it had been home to the so-called marathon monks. Not only were they highly trained warriors, they also believed that they could reach enlightenment by following a discipline of daily running exercises. No wonder I struggle with how religions have developed.

But there were also serene temples and meditation gardens up there. In the gardens, parts were filled with moss, making the visitor reflect on decay, parts were made up of raked sand that would soon be disturbed by the wind and rain, reminding the visitor to focus on the moment rather than the future, and parts were shaped into cones to reflect moonlight into the temple. Temple gardens are all about inner and outer reflection…

One of the following evenings held something very special: a Japanese Reiki Share organised by Hyakuten Inamoto, the Buddhist monk and Reiki teacher. A Reiki Share is a meeting of practitioners to give one another Reiki. After some meandering through tiny side-streets, I eventually found the place, a little temple right in the centre of Kyoto. 'Finally, real Japanese Reiki,' I thought.

But actually it was just a normal Reiki Share. Reiki is Reiki, wherever you are. The techniques may vary slightly, that's all. This Reiki Share was a brilliant reminder of that. Twenty people participated, first receiving *Reiju* (a Reiki blessing), then taking part in a group treatment. Three people received Reiki simultaneously on treatment couches and after about 20 minutes it was somebody else's turn. Not everyone received a treatment, though I was kindly invited to have one.

The most amazing experience wasn't the Reiki Share itself, but meeting someone who took part. When I asked whether anyone spoke English, a lady of Japanese appearance with a rather growling voice said, 'I do... I'm American... My name is Phyllis.'

When I heard that, I immediately had an idea of who she might be, but wanted to be sure and asked for her surname.

'Furumoto,' she said promptly.

Yes, she was the granddaughter of Hawayo Takata, the lady who was single-handedly responsible for spreading Reiki to all four corners of the world! Phyllis had become her successor as the head of Usui Shiki Ryoho, a western Reiki tradition.

That was the only Reiki Share I was able to attend in Japan, and even though she had been in Kyoto for several weeks, it was the only one she was able to make too. There was no way that could have been a coincidence. But what was it supposed to tell me? Maybe that it doesn't matter whether you learn Reiki in Japan or elsewhere, it is always the same. And if you are meant to meet someone, the universe will arrange it – even in the most unexpected of places.

22.

Kurama Again

I had to go to Mount Kurama again. There was something, I thought, that I hadn't found. Back on the subway, then the little Keihan Railway … and there I was again, being greeted by the red hobgoblin.

Walking up the mountain, this time I strayed a bit more to the left and right, finding even more temples, shrines and lantern-flanked paths. Everything was painted orange and beautifully kept. But why would Mikao Usui have chosen this place for his fasting retreat? Why not a cave somewhere? Or a proper mountain? Why not Mt Hiei?

I walked past the places that were familiar from my previous visit and tried to meditate in front of the Buddha again, but felt rather uncomfortable when I was joined by gigantic beetles crawling all over the floor. There was definitely a theme going on with insects and meditation.

Finally, I arrived at the main hall, this time determined to find the crypt. Hidden from public view, there was a staircase on either side of the altar. Downstairs, a large room was lit with candles, and as my eyes became accustomed to the light, I became aware of hundreds of small urns. For 20,000 Yen, anyone could buy an urn, put a lock of their hair inside and place it in the crypt. Monks would then pray once a day for them.

I felt so uncomfortable that I had to leave quickly. Paying for other people to pray for you? To get in the front row in heaven? Something didn't sound right there.

Five hundred years ago, something similar was going on in Germany: people could pay the Church to have their sins forgiven. If, obviously, they had the means. Everyone else had to work a bit harder. Martin Luther found this scheme, designed to finance the building of churches, including St Peter's in Rome, so repulsive that it inspired him to start what we now call the Reformation. An interesting connection.

Beyond the main hall, Mount Kurama gets a bit wilder. Instead of stone steps there are just paths, at times rather steep ones. Visitors are greeted by a big yellow warning sign showing snakes, mosquitoes, deer and bears. Each year, I subsequently learned, dozens of people are killed by bears in the Japanese mountains.

After about 15 minutes of climbing, you reach the top of the mountain and the atmosphere changes completely. Suddenly you feel very exposed. The wind hits you sharply and it feels significantly colder. In the winter, there can be snow and ice up there. And there are many exposed roots on the ground.

The strange, unwelcoming energy of the mountain adds to the unsettling experience. The pleasant confines of the temple complex are behind you; now you are on your own.

I began to understand that this was exactly the experience Mikao Usui had been looking for.

Walking around, I almost repeated another of his experiences by catching my toe on a root. I took that as a sign that I was at the very spot where it had all happened – the struggle, the enlightenment and the first healing experience.

Later, when I looked at my pictures of that day, I realised that I had captured a ray of light shining through the trees. And an orb. The first I had ever photographed.

23.

1710

All in all, it had been a pretty amazing journey. But somehow I still felt the big breakthrough hadn't materialized. I began to resign myself to the idea that it wasn't meant to be.

At least I'd had enough experiences and encounters to make the trip worthwhile – and taken so many photographs that I'd have website illustrations for the rest of my life. Incidentally, by now I'd heeded my grandfather's advice and taken a computer course, and had been creating all my own marketing literature and even my own websites. And now I had no shortage of material.

To complete the sightseeing, I packed as much as possible into the last day. But I certainly wasn't prepared for the dynamics that developed.

At 8 a.m., the taxi arrived to take me to the Zen temple for morning meditation. I wanted to experience Zazen again. On the way there we were caught in traffic and I glimpsed the number plate of the bus stopping in front of us. It showed the number 1710.

To most people, I suppose, that number would be meaningless. But for me it is special: my birthday is on 17 October – 17.10 in the European form of the date. Was this a coincidence?

When I arrived at the temple, I looked at the meter on the taxi and had to laugh out loud. The price was 1,710 Yen! No coincidence then – that much was clear. Obviously this journey had some significance for my life path.

Before the meditation, I was able to ask the vice-abbot a few questions about life in a monastery in the early twentieth century. When I told him that my questions related to a man called Mikao Usui, he wasn't surprised. Reiki students had apparently already been visiting his temple to find out more about the connection between Zen Buddhism and Usui. But the friendly expression had vanished from his face. The students had obviously annoyed him. And, he told me, his subsequent enquiries into Mikao Usui, with a number of other monasteries in Kyoto, had revealed that he hadn't just joined one monastery, but three, and had been thrown out of all of them.

We couldn't continue the conversation as the meditation was about to start, but my head was swirling. During the meditation, I went through what I had learned about Mikao Usui. And suddenly something stood out: prison. Several accounts, including those by Hawayo Takata, mention that Usui either worked as a missionary or a social worker in prisons. I had always wondered about this recurring detail, but never followed it up. After all, how could I have done so? But now it became clear to me that he might have done some missionary work in a prison because he had *been in prison*.

After Zazen I had the opportunity to speak to the vice-abbot again, but I didn't mention my sudden intuition. However, reminiscing for a while on the information he had received, he suddenly, completely unprompted, said, 'Personally, I believe that Mikao Usui spent time in jail.'

I just said, 'Yes, I actually think so too.'

I left with a feeling of incredible relief. I felt that finally the truth was coming out.

I was certain that more people had known about this, but had diplomatically glossed over it. But doesn't it make the development of Reiki even more amazing? That somebody with such a background could transform so much that he experienced a moment of enlightenment – and gave the world its most amazing spiritual healing system?

I spent the rest of the day rushing from temple to temple to make sure I had seen most of the important sights, but my mind was only occupied with what I had come across that morning. What was I supposed to do with the information? How could I get independent proof?

And something else was odd, too: I was on my own. Ever since my visit to his grave, I had somehow been aware of Mikao Usui's presence. Now I didn't feel anything; it was as if he had gone into hiding. It reminded me of a few days earlier, when my Japanese guide had been a few minutes late for our meeting and been silent for a significant while because he was embarrassed. Hours later, he had suddenly muttered, 'Sorry I was late this morning.'

A similar dynamic may have been in play, because in the afternoon, the familiar voice came back.

Mikao Usui said, 'Now you know.'

Why did this happen on the very last day of my trip? To me, there was only one obvious answer: the journey was to be continued.

Three months later, I was back.

24.

Japan and Back

Looking back now, that last day in Kyoto almost feels like a trick to lure me back. This trip would have even more unexpected events. Far more. In comparison, I suppose it would be fair to say that the first trip was nothing but a warm-up exercise.

This time, I started in Kyoto. With a clear mission: finding evidence for the rumours that Mikao Usui had been in three monasteries – and in prison. As a non-Japanese speaker in a notoriously private society, I was facing what could have seemed an impossible task. But why had I been given these leads, if I wasn't meant to follow them up? And Hyakuten Inamoto, a native speaker, had offered to help.

Flicking through my Kyoto guidebook to prepare for the trip, I had found one place standing out: a temple called Shoren-in. There was no reason to go there other than intuition, but that was enough. That was where I would start. Not only was it beautiful and tranquil, as are most temples in Kyoto, but it also turned out that it ranked very highly in the hierarchy of Buddhist monasteries because of its close connection with the Japanese royal family.

Not that that always guarantees privileges. I later heard that a few decades ago a member of the royal family decided to join the monastery and everybody was very excited because they thought that with this guy would come substantial financial subsidies. When he arrived, however, he said something along the lines of

'I'm now an ordinary monk,' renounced the luxury of the court and lived humbly for the rest of his life. There were no financial rewards whatsoever.

When I arrived in Japan, Hyakuten Inamoto wasn't free for another week. Why not just go to the monastery by myself?

Shoren-in was situated in a particularly beautiful location in the foothills of a range of mountains, with many other temples nearby. Unlike the other temples, though, it had a rather large forecourt which was used as a car park. It wasn't very busy, so I walked past the cars and through the gate.

What stood out to me were the large trees overhanging parts of the forecourt and, as with so many temples, that the actual building almost seemed to be floating. It was raised on wooden stilts with a gap of about three feet underneath to keep it safe from flooding (Kyoto has extraordinary amounts of rainfall) and the unwelcome visits of animals. This also eliminated the need to wear shoes, which were taken off right at the entrance – I recommend shoes without laces if you visit Japan, as you are constantly taking them on and off – and provided the interesting feeling of never being quite grounded, of floating above the gardens.

I walked through the different rooms, some interconnecting, others accessed via the long balconies surrounding most of the temple and doubling as corridors. They invited you to meditate, contemplate or simply absorb the peace and calm, even though the vast majority of visitors didn't seem to do so. On my two trips to Japan, I hardly ever saw a visitor who seemed to be there for spiritual reasons. They were all looking at the religious sights with the same interest they would have shown for the Eiffel Tower: a beautiful building, but nothing to do with me.

Although the Shoren-in temple gardens were accessible and offered lovely meditative paths, they were also designed to be viewed from inside the temple, with the sliding doors providing ever-changing angles of contemplation.

I was particularly taken by a little courtyard with an old cherry tree. At that time of year it was bare, but its shiny silver-coloured bark looked as if it was reflecting moonlight. The thick, crooked branches also made the tree look like the perfect sculpture for contemplating age.

But I wasn't there for contemplation, but for research. And once again I was feeling the presence of Mikao Usui. Was he indeed connected with this temple?

Gathering all my courage together, I walked back to the reception area and asked whether anybody spoke English. And yes, somebody did! After what seemed to be a search of the entire office, a young man appeared and offered his help.

I explained that I was researching a historical person called Mikao Usui, who was said to have been connected with this monastery. Would they be able to check?

The young man seemed a bit hesitant and disappeared into the back room. A while later, he came back to inform me that they didn't have a record of that name. But they didn't have historical records there, anyway – they were kept at the headquarters near Mount Hiei.

Well, that hadn't quite worked out as expected. But I had another week to go. And a lead.

The following morning the jetlag was kicking in badly, and I woke up at 5.40 a.m. I tried to get back to sleep, but couldn't. Instead, I must have entered a semi-conscious state. I remember feeling a strange sensation in my throat, as if something was expanding, and began to see what looked like a film-clip: two men were rushing across the forecourt of the Shoren-in temple. I could only see their backs and they seemed in a hurry. But what stuck in my mind was their clothing – the intense colours of their elegant robes and their strangely shaped triangular sleeves. They oozed importance and it felt as if they had urgent business at the monastery.

Suddenly, it seemed to me that I was one of them. The scene had the familiarity of a past-life regression.

So that was why I felt so attached to Kyoto: I had lived there in a past life! What had happened then? It didn't feel as though I had been a priest or someone living at the monastery. It felt as if I had been a scholar, a person who had commanded respect, whose advice had been sought. I got a sense of entitlement and arrogance, but also of intelligence and knowledge.

And then it dawned on me that this was the early twentieth century! I had lived in Kyoto at the time of Mikao Usui. And briefly met him.

Met him? As soon as that idea came into my mind, I was wide awake. Had I been dreaming? But I knew I hadn't. I'd had so many past-life regressions by then that I couldn't argue it away. It had all the hallmarks of one.

How I wished I'd had a therapist guiding me through that scene – perhaps then I wouldn't have come out of it so quickly. It felt as if I'd only got half of the story.

Looking for proof, I subsequently tried to find examples of Japanese robes with triangular sleeves, but all I found were rectangular ones. Then, several days later, I saw a priest in a traditional robe walking down the road in front of me. His sleeves were rectangular – until he started to walk faster. Then they suddenly appeared to be triangular.

Still a bit dazed by my early-morning experience, I had to get ready: today was another bank holiday – the Meiji Emperor's birthday – and I was due to meet Michi at 10 a.m. and spend the day in Nara.

From a tourist's point of view, this would definitely have been one of the highlights of the trip: the ancient capital of Japan, with its giant temples in a vast deer park. The Emperor had resided here until he had escaped the pressure of the clergy by relocating to Kyoto. For hundreds of years, these temples hadn't been touched and they simply exuded history and grandeur ... and the power of religion.

I got several very touristy pictures of myself feeding the deer and had the best Japanese lunch ever – an entire tray filled with vegetarian dishes. I ate every scrap. And yet I spent most of my time in Nara in kind of a daze, just thinking about my early-morning experience.

Was I actually connected to Mikao Usui's time in the monastery? And was that a good thing or a bad thing? I was uneasy

– something didn't feel right. Just as it didn't feel right to see a small hole in a pillar in a huge temple in Nara and be told that it was believed that you could attain enlightenment by crawling through it. I wondered whether my role had been as unholy as such ridiculous ideas.

My favourite discovery in Nara, though, happened on the way back, when Michi and I passed a small crowd that had gathered around a street vendor. When I asked my friend what it was all about, he just disappeared, and five minutes later came back with the sweetest sweet I had ever tasted: a freshly made, gooey mochi ball.

Unlike the hole in the temple pillar, this *was* the way to heaven. At least temporarily.

25.

Fudo Myo-o

Reading my story again, I realise that I must come across as pretty ungrateful: Reiki had got me out of the most difficult period of my life, I had become a successful Reiki teacher, gained the most amazing insights through past-life regression and mediumship, and come across previously unknown information about the history of Reiki. Now I had a past-life memory actively connecting me with the founder of the system. What more did I want?

Well, I wanted proof. And I was getting increasingly frustrated. I couldn't just go home and tell people that I had new information about the history of Reiki, based on hearsay and intuition. As beautiful as Kyoto was, I wasn't there for sightseeing or mochi balls.

The next morning, I decided to try another avenue – the one that had basically started this whole second journey. I took a taxi to the monastery where I'd had the conversation with the vice-abbot.

He was there again to greet the visitors and he recognized me. He didn't appear particularly pleased to see me, though.

It turned out that he had actually looked at my book – not really reading it, but flicking through it. What had stood out for him were the symbols. And he had been appalled: they didn't look Japanese at all! Admittedly, they had been drawn with a felt pen

154

rather than a brush, but apart from that, they were just as originally designed. But he didn't recognise them as part of a 'classic tradition' and therefore decided to dismiss them. I suspected he simply hadn't seen them before. But his view was that if the symbols weren't traditionally Japanese, the rest of the system couldn't be either. That was basically it. He had no intention of taking the conversation further.

There was no way I could explain that the whole point of the symbols – and system – was not to be specifically Japanese, but to be usable for everyone, no matter what their cultural background.

He did, however, confirm what I'd been assuming for a long time: that the three Reiki symbols for the second-level training had been created specifically for Reiki, and not, as claimed by so many Reiki teachers, rediscovered in ancient scriptures.

Other than that, I can't say that I felt particularly encouraged as I left the monastery. What next?

So far, all I had was an obscure past-life connection to the temple of Shoren-in. They may not have had a record of Mikao Usui there, but they apparently had a famous painting that I hadn't seen last time, a 12th-century painting of the Blue Fudo Myo-o that was one of the oldest images of that Buddhist deity. As I had no other plans, I decided to go back and see it.

I walked up to the familiar reception again, this time enquiring where I would find the famous painting, only to be told that it wasn't actually there but in a sub-temple up the hill.

Assuming the bus driver wouldn't speak English, I wasn't brave enough to take the bus, so I went on an hour-long hike.

For the view alone, it was worth it: the newly renovated sub-temple was built on a plateau with the most magnificent views that revealed that Kyoto was actually located in a valley surrounded by a number of mountain ranges.

At the temple, I paid my admission fee and entered a rather bare hall. It had all the charm of a multi-function community centre.

In one corner there was an entrance to a smaller room, which housed the famous painting. I sat down in front of it and looked at it. For five minutes, ten minutes, half an hour. The picture was mesmerising and somehow mirrored how I felt: uneasy, unhappy, unpleasant.

His skin painted a deep blue, Fudo Myo-o was sitting on a rock surrounded by raging flames, holding a lasso in one hand and a sword in the other. He was distinctly ugly and his expression fearsome.

Fudo means 'the unmovable' and points to the unpleasant truth that challenges in life are inevitable. The sword represents chopping the ego away, the lasso catching unhelpful desires, and the flames burning away the distractions, while the essence of a human being is safely seated on a rock-solid foundation. The often-overlooked lotus flower on Fudo Myo-o's head symbolises that all the challenges are a sign of universal love and are meant to help us focus on the experience of truth inside, rather than feel lost in the outer world's challenges.

Suddenly I realized that this frustrating morning, indeed the past frustrating couple of days, had been like this very fire, burning away ... my ego. I had wanted to follow up this new information about Mikao Usui. I had been amazed to have been given this lead. I had thought it would be fascinating to reveal the information to the world. But to be honest, *why*? Who would benefit from it? Who would benefit from knowing more about Usui's life *before* he founded the system of Reiki?

To be sure, it would have been very interesting, but maybe my journey wasn't about that at all.

But if not, what *was* it about? Did everything *have* to have a purpose anyway? Maybe I was just meant to have an interesting experience. Maybe I just had to accept that there wasn't any further information.

After all, Reiki would still work. And that was the only thing that really mattered.

Maybe I should just send my ego on holiday, enjoy Japan and leave everything to the universe. Hadn't I learned to trust it by now?

I suddenly realised that this long thought process had been made possible by the newly installed underfloor heating. Ha! There were certainly worse places to be right now.

In a way, I surrendered. Accepted that I wasn't in charge anymore.

Then it came.

It wasn't a voice, rather an intuition, an inner knowing:

A hundred years ago, when I lived in Japan, I was a scholar, a lay priest, from a well-off background. I was intelligent, arrogant – and helped to kick Mikao Usui out of the monastery.

I came back to relive Usui's experiences: religion, politics, entrepreneurship, bankruptcy, losing friends and family, wanting to die, or contemplating desperate things to survive.

I also became aware of how deeply traditional Japanese religion and culture were engrained in Mikao Usui, as shown by his donation of a gate for the Shinto shrine in his birthplace, Taniai. But Reiki needed to be taken out of Japanese confines. That was why I had been reborn in the West.

Wow. That was quite a bit of information. As I let it slowly sink in, I started to wonder whether it was just my imagination going into overdrive. It felt true. But could it be?

I must have been sitting there for almost an hour, cross-legged the whole time, and when I finally disentangled my legs and got up, resting for a while to ease the numbness, I noticed a donation box in the room. Although I didn't really feel very material at that moment, I reluctantly felt compelled to reach into my pocket. Quite a bit of change had accumulated there over the course of the day, and I took out a selection to see what to use.

When I looked into my palm, any doubts disappeared. I had pulled out three coins: 1, 10 and 100 Yen – 111 in total.

Confirmation? For me, it was.

I began to wonder why I had planned to spend another two days in Tokyo, but the hotel was booked, so I went.

Even after a week, I was still feeling jetlagged, and was much more awake at night than during the day. So I dived into the nightlife. Two days of proper holidays! I met some lovely people and had some interesting conversations. Eventually I confided my frustration about my lack of progress in validating the rumours about Mikao Usui to a university student who happened to sit next to me in a crowded bar. He had an interesting and very matter-of-fact view on why there was so much hesitancy about sharing information: privacy laws.

A few years earlier, Japan had introduced a new swathe of these laws, making it virtually impossible to get any information about anyone, alive or dead. The student told me that there had been a famous case concerning a young man who had wanted to find more about his grandfather, who had died during World War II. He was denied the information on the grounds of not being the son, but a later generation.

The conversation ended with the suggestion that there was little hope of me – or indeed anyone – getting the information I was after. That wasn't very encouraging, but at least it was an explanation.

I went back to Kyoto and looked forward to something that was at least guaranteed to bring tangible results: visiting Taniai, Mikao Usui's birthplace. Another photo opportunity.

26.

'That's Why I'm Telling You This'

And now we are back at the beginning… Mikao Usui. Sitting on the stone, smiling.

The first thought that came into my mind was that he was actually rather handsome. (How ridiculous is that?!) He appeared to be in his thirties and was dressed in a formal style, looking very different from the familiar images of an older and much fatter man that I had seen in books. But there was no mistaking who he was.

'I knew this would get your attention,' he joked.

Then he started to explain my life to me. He talked about my religious childhood, my stint in the army and politics, my career as an entrepreneur, my bankruptcy, homelessness, struggle to feed myself and desire to end it all. And he said that it had all been my own choice. It had all been to help me learn more humility, he said, to get beyond the arrogant achiever's outlook on life that I used to have.

Confirming my intuition of a few days earlier, he told me, 'You throwing me out of the monastery – the final straw before I went to Mt Kurama – was all part of the plan for that lifetime. When we were both back in the spirit world, we decided that you would go through the same experiences to understand the foundations on which Reiki was built – and how non-judgemental it is.'

'We' – that meant me and *him*.

I had so many questions and he was happy to answer them. Yes, he had also had a very religious childhood – he showed me an image of him as a small boy listening to the priests in the temple in Taniai. When he grew up, he was a bit of a ladies' man, he confirmed, with a twinkle in his eye. And yes, he had remained closely connected to the Earth plane ever since his passing to support the development of Reiki.

He explained that he'd already had many previous incarnations as a spiritual teacher, mainly in the East, and they had been necessary for him to achieve all that he had.

'Everything we do builds up over several lives.'

He confirmed that I'd had a few lifetimes as a spiritual teacher myself, often in France, and that was why I had such a connection to that area.

I feel a bit embarrassed that I asked whether it was okay for me to still design jewellery alongside practising Reiki. All this and I was still struggling to accept my path!

He said, 'Yes, no problem at all. We will make sure that it doesn't become too overwhelming for you. But just to be clear: *you aren't here for that; you're here for something else.*'

He told me I would focus on Reiki more and more and enjoy it. I was on the right path with my understanding of the importance of the three levels of existence to which the Reiki symbols were gateways.

He showed me that Reiki would become more important in the future, not just for me but for the world, and that we needed it, as more and more of us were becoming disconnected from nature and from spirituality.

'Take Reiki into the cities,' he said again and again. 'Take Reiki into the cities.'

It needed to become part of normal, busy, everyday life.

Throughout the conversation, I felt loved and supported and appreciated his wonderfully dry sense of humour. He was actually very, very human, which explains, I suppose, why the Reiki system is as approachable as it is.

'Don't worry,' he said, 'you are very much on the right path and I am by your side. I will guide you.'

He smiled.

Then he said those words that have stayed with me: 'You will bring Reiki into the 21st century.'

And disappeared.

I remember that I was so puzzled that I couldn't even feel excited. How was I supposed to bring Reiki into the 21st century? And of course, doubts came up immediately too. Had I been dreaming? Was I making things up? Was I losing my mind?

'Calm down,' I told myself. 'You're not a fantasist. You have a master's degree in a scientific discipline. You like facts. You planned this trip to get proper historical evidence. Didn't you?'

Yes, I did. And instead, I had a chat with a spirit.

Just moments later, Michi came over to let me know it was time to leave. We went back to the hotel for dinner – a traditional dinner of at least 15 courses, although some of them were served together. But while I was eating, there was only one thought in my head: 'Did that really just happen?!'

Even though I had learned so much over the years and had so many experiences, I was dead scared – and, finally, incredibly excited at the same time.

And of course the Meiji Emperor's poem came back into my mind:

If we falter in resolve
just because the task is hard,
no accomplishment can follow...

But how could I possibly tell others about this experience? Wouldn't I have to face a barrage of ridicule? When I had asked Mikao Usui whether I should share it, he'd just replied, 'Of course – that's why I'm telling you this!'

For a long time, though, I didn't tell anyone. With the exception of Mum, of course. I wasn't ready. And as for bringing Reiki into the 21st century, wasn't it there already?

Unsurprisingly, there weren't any more major new insights during my remaining time in Japan. The next day, Michi and I visited Taniai as planned and had a chat with the wife of Mikao Usui's sister's grandson, who had only recently learned about his famous ancestor.

I also heard about the story of Usui's younger brother, who, after retiring as a policeman, returned to Taniai and attuned several people to Reiki. So his brother must have initiated him as a Reiki Master too.

One of the people he had attuned still lived in Taniai and some Japanese Reiki Masters had interviewed him about the early days of Reiki teaching. Sadly, the man, now in his late eighties, couldn't remember anything except that he had received healing hands. He had been eight years old at the time.

More and more I was realising that investigating the past was the wrong approach. Hadn't Mikao Usui himself just told me to look to the future?

I still didn't give up on historical information, though, and went to the central administration of the Buddhist Tendai tradition with my friend the Buddhist monk to see if they had any records of an obnoxious monk called Mikao Usui.

We were politely asked to wait in reception, then told they didn't have a record of anyone of that name. Something more must have been going on, though, that I didn't understand, as my friend suddenly appeared rather nervous and quickly left the building. Had he crossed cultural boundaries?

Or was it that he just hadn't been pushy enough? Determined to try another approach, I returned two days later on my own, explaining that I was doing research for a book and had come all the way from Europe. But 15 minutes later, the polite gentleman I had spoken to returned and told me that they had no record of Mikao Usui in their database. However, not all the names connected with the individual monasteries had been transferred from the written accounts to the database. My heart leapt – but then I was informed that they couldn't currently access the remaining written records.

I was disappointed, but my friend the monk didn't regard the historical information as central anyway. He was much more interested in how I practised Reiki.

'How do you bring it into your life?' he asked. 'How does it *change* your life? How do you teach the students to change *their* lives?'

And he was so right. Reiki isn't about one man's history, but about many people's lives. I could have learned that anywhere, but I chose Japan.

Now there was only one real question: how to bring Reiki into the 21st century?

Part III

The Universe

27.

Dad

Back in London, I wasn't any the wiser. My Reiki courses and workshops were more popular than ever and I was being invited to give public talks on Reiki. I was adding more spiritual content than ever before. But was I really doing anything new? What *should* I be doing?

I began work on a new book, but became overwhelmed by other demands. Dad hadn't been well for a while. He had suffered from prostate cancer for several years and it had now spread. When his back pain became unbearable, the doctors found tumours in his spine. When his leg fractured in several places, they found tumours there. His bravery was incredible. Mine wasn't. I couldn't bear to see him suffer. Every few weeks I flew over to Germany and in between trips I tried to organise his healthcare remotely.

He had one operation after another: metal rods inserted into his spine, clamps put into his legs and glue placed anywhere from bones to bladder and intestines. The doctors kept being amazed by how quickly he recovered after the surgery and how quickly the wounds healed. Of course I was sending Reiki every time. But the cancer kept on spreading.

One evening, when I had just left the hospital and gone to have something to eat in the Spanish restaurant next door, I couldn't cope any longer. I started to argue with the universe: '*Why* is he getting worse and worse? I don't want him to die! I want him around for longer!'

To my surprise, I actually received an answer: '*You* want him to stay. It's not about him, it's about you. You must allow him what is right for him.'

It was hard, but I began to do this.

I still hoped that he would hang on for as long he could possibly bear, but began to accept that it was his own journey. It was an interesting realisation: I had all this spiritual understanding and deep trust that life didn't end with death, yet I still wanted to postpone Dad's transition for as long as possible. It's not easy to let go.

After a few months, he had stabilised enough to be at home for a while, looked after by his second wife. I rented a little country cottage for a few weeks to continue working on my book, but it obviously wasn't the right time. After just a fortnight, Mum phoned.

A few days before, I had been thinking about a minor problem she had with her ears. Sitting in meditation, I suddenly heard someone saying, 'She only needs surgery, then it will all be fine.' Surgery? *Mum*? That couldn't be true.

In fact her ears turned out to be perfectly fine. She was phoning about something else. A routine examination of a very different organ had uncovered the fact that she had cancer.

I packed everything in my car and three hours later I was home. Not cancer again!

Dad was getting stronger and stronger, so, weirdly, we could concentrate on Mum. She had surgery within weeks, two days before Christmas Eve, and indeed that was all she needed. No chemotherapy, no further treatment. Just loads of Reiki.

At the end of January, she was well enough to be left on her own for a few days, and I could join the retreat with Neale Donald Walsch and finally tell him in person how his book had saved me from suicide and given me hope. Then the organisers asked me to run the following retreat a few months later. What an honour to follow in his footsteps...

But within days, Dad's condition deteriorated, and on the last day of the retreat, I booked a flight to Hamburg. It seems I had been given a five-day window to attend the retreat and now it was time to turn to family matters again.

When I arrived, Dad didn't recognise me. The morphine had taken over. My loving, joyful, active father had been reduced to a pain-ridden, unresponsive shell.

He was moved to a hospice, and my stepmother and I visited him every day. Each time I gave him Reiki, and to my great delight now and then he briefly opened his eyes and even said my name. But most of the time he was already far away.

One morning, about two weeks later, was different. Even on the way to the hospice we could feel it. It was as if the universe was preparing us. When we approached his room, I knew that something had changed. I opened the door – and there was ... *light*. Along the wall I could see something that could best be described as a presence of light – a group of light, a group of people in spirit. I was sure they had come to welcome Dad.

My stepmother and I sat down by his side and held his hands. He was clearly in great pain and it was simply unbearable to look at him. All I hoped was that his suffering would end soon!

I had been told that dying people often don't want to let go of their loved ones on Earth, so my stepmother and I decided to tell him that it was okay to go. In the end we were so assertive that we almost told him off for still clinging on to life! But his breathing was rapidly becoming more laboured and it was clear that he didn't have long.

From time to time, I looked to the side. The people of light were slowly coming closer. After what must have been 20 or 30 minutes, they arrived at the foot of the bed. Simultaneously Dad's breathing became shallower and shallower. Although I could see individual beings in the spirit group, I couldn't make out any faces. But I sensed that Dad's mother and grandmother were among them. I could feel them there.

One of them eventually leaned forward and stretched out her hand, as if to give Dad something to hold on to and take him to the other side.

Seconds later, he took his last breath.

What happened next was something that is as difficult to put into words as it is hilarious: I felt they were having a welcome party on the other side! Everything felt positive, happy and filled with light … and I was sitting there thinking, 'Why isn't anyone concerned about *me*? I just lost my dad!' But then the most unexpected of feelings swept through me: I was happy.

Suddenly I thought: 'I know where Dad is going! I know he is in safe hands. And in a better place.'

Just two days later, I was able to teach another Reiki course.

28.

Going Digital

More and more of my students were telling me that they had seen Reiki courses offered online and asking for my opinion of them. It wasn't very high. When I checked out what was on offer, I found some courses had the basic information, but certainly didn't venture into the spiritual aspects of Reiki, and most were the very opposite of inspirational.

My publishers had already asked me for a Reiki online course to complement my first book. I reluctantly agreed, on condition that it didn't include an attunement, so it really was just an introduction to Reiki rather than a proper course.

But it got me thinking... Online courses would be able to reach more people, probably many more – those who couldn't take a weekend off due to family or work, those in remote locations, those confined to their homes (which happened a few years later through covid, on a much bigger scale than ever anticipated).

I bought a camcorder, which even then was rather outdated, and searched for a computer teacher who could show Mum and me how to do it all ourselves: Mum behind the camera and me delivering the content and then editing it with online software. After all, the internet was full of such videos (though maybe not with the mother behind the camera).

To describe the results as 'semi-professional' would be something of an exaggeration. They were much worse than that. But Ryan, the young man I hired as a computer teacher, was brilliant with just about every aspect involved – filming, editing, sound – so he took over and became my videographer. I think the universe sent him to me! He got such a clear idea of what I wanted to put across that he helped to market the course too. Today, he is a Reiki Master and a good friend.

It took over six months to film Reiki 1 and 2, with 72 individual videos and a total running time of 15 hours. The biggest problem was ensuring a respectful approach to the attunements. But of course I had already attuned Tanja distantly, even while she was driving! And I had sent an attunement to Dad, who, in a possible a past-life memory, had seen himself surrounded by Buddhist monks in orange clothing.

Each online student could book their individual slot for an attunement, and connecting with them became part of my daily routine. I would send the attunements from wherever I happened to be. Once I found my brother-in-law rather puzzled when, just before Sunday lunch, he asked where I was and Mum told him I'd just nipped somewhere quiet to give a few attunements...

The feedback was so overwhelming that I was actually rather embarrassed that I had waited such a long time before offering an online course. But maybe it was necessary to get it to the standard that I wanted.

And it turned out that it didn't make much of a difference whether a course was delivered online or in person. To my surprise, many people taking the online course had already trained in Reiki and were looking to deepen their knowledge. I was really touched when one student commented: 'No books, no other courses have taken me as deep into Reiki as Torsten's course.'

Within the Reiki community, though, online courses remained something of a divisive issue. Particularly opposed was one tradition that also insisted on Reiki being taught solely as an oral tradition: students were neither given manuals nor allowed to take any notes. The argument that it might be difficult to remember the symbols correctly wasn't accepted, and when I dared to refer to the symbols in a public talk, I was shunned by most of the audience for the rest of the convention – much to my surprise, as I wasn't aware that they all came from that Reiki tradition.

As much as I understand the need to preserve and respect the original teachings, orthodoxy can sometimes hinder progress. It is only because one person, Usui's Master student Chujiro Hayashi, broke free of the rigid confines of the original Reiki teaching organisation, the Gakkai, in the 1930s that we have Reiki in the world today.

29.

Montserrat

There is definitely something about mountains! In most spiritual and religious traditions, they play a major role as places of breakthrough. Much to my surprise, a mountain also played that role for me.

At the retreat with Neale Donald Walsch, when I was asked if I would run the next one, I was thrilled. The organisers, the renowned spiritual event organisers Alternatives, had already offered me the opportunity to give talks in London, joining a list of speakers that included Mother Teresa and the Dalai Lama. They told me they had been looking for a Reiki speaker for a decade, and I was the first they had asked. And now a five-day retreat... Of course I wanted to meet their expectations, and those of the participants, who would be travelling from all over the world, so I spent months preparing.

A few weeks before the retreat, I met my psychic friend Stewart Pearce, who gave me an interesting prediction. Three things would happen: a monk would say something important to me; the retreat would eventually turn into a book; and I would have an experience that he could only describe as 'seeing light'. Stewart is a remarkable intuitive, so my expectations for the retreat went through the roof. As did my nervousness.

The date for the retreat was moved several times until it finally fitted in with everybody's schedule. The final start date meant that

I would arrive on my birthday, and I remember being asked whether that would be okay. Of course I said it was perfectly fine. At the time I didn't realise I was being given a sign. There it was again, my birth date: 1710.

The mountain of Montserrat, an unusual rock formation arising from a much flatter landscape, is home to the medieval monastery of the same name. Just under an hour's drive from Barcelona, the capital of the state of Catalunya in north-eastern Spain, it houses a statue of the Black Madonna, Catalunya's patron saint. Originally hard to reach, today it is accessible to the hundreds of thousands of worshippers and tourists who come each year via cable car, funicular, a train or car. I suppose some might even hike. No matter how you get there, it is worth it. Pilgrims have been going there for over a thousand years.

I arrived feeling daunted by the responsibility I had taken on. Would my retreat be good enough? Would it be deep enough? Would it be what people expected? Or hoped for? Would it bring *change*?

I only managed to sleep for about two hours that first night, and the next morning my mind was swirling. Normally, my courses had a very clear structure. And over the years, I'd built up enough experience to pretty much deal with any question that arose. But this was new territory. Suddenly I was asking myself, 'Who are you to think that you can do something new with Reiki, which has been around for almost 100 years?'

As the hotel was part of the monastery, guests had special early-morning access to the church, and I felt a few moments of meditation might help me. I walked up to the balcony that housed the statue of the Black Madonna and, to my surprise, felt calmer. Just like the statue of Amida Nyorai on Mt Kurama, the Madonna felt like a portal to higher vibrations. Centuries of over-eager polishing had darkened the wood dramatically and given the statue its name, but the artwork was superb, and it may well be that the artist had managed to capture divine qualities. The accumulation of hope, trust and spiritual energy from millions of visitors may also have played a part, but either way there was definitely a presence around the statue. I hoped this would allow me to regain my equilibrium.

I left the cathedral and was walking back across the atrium, a square courtyard surrounded by arched columns, when I noticed a group of probably Japanese tourists posing for pictures in the middle. Somehow, I felt drawn to this central point. I waited a few minutes until all the selfies and group pictures had been taken and then walked to the spot where a tile marked the centre of the square.

As soon as I stood there and closed my eyes, something started to happen in my body. My feet felt rooted to the ground as if there were giant magnets beneath them, holding and grounding me in a way I had never experienced before. I had the feeling that I was becoming one with the earth.

Then I felt a pulling sensation on the top of my head as if I was being lifted up and connected with the light above me. It was as if I was on a journey to higher levels in the universe, but at the same time completely grounded on the physical plane.

179

All I could see was light. The brightest ever.

I don't know how long I stood there, maybe five minutes, maybe ten, but I just didn't want to move. For the first time, I felt that it was possible to be both completely human and completely spirit, and to be in complete harmony.

The best way to describe it is probably to say that I felt oneness. Oneness and happiness.

I never wanted it to end, but eventually I became aware that another group of tourists was moving closer in the hope of another set of pictures, so I left the spot, moved into the shade of the cloisters and shed tears of happiness, relief and gratitude.

Oneness.

That was what the retreat was all about. This was what life was all about. That was the only truth in the universe.

Looking back, it feels just as surreal as it did then. And I am very much aware that it was only a moment and that the ups and downs of life have continued ever since. But it was a moment of sudden understanding. Of change.

In Japanese, a moment of *satori*.

I still wonder whether there is an energy centre that the monastery's architects cleverly identified and built the atrium around, or whether it is the architecture itself, aided by the accumulated energy of spiritual seekers over the centuries that makes that spot so special. The particular formation of serrated rocks, remarkably similar to those surrounding the Valley of the Kings in Egypt, may also be a factor.

There is one thing I am sure of, though: at that moment, I had given up. I had realised that I couldn't do things on my own anymore. I had surrendered. Just like Mikao Usui on Mt Kurama.

There was no way I could face the course participants in the condition I was in, so I texted the organisers and asked for their understanding if I was 15 minutes late.

Of course, I then started the day by relating the experience – as well as I was able – and the rest of the retreat naturally followed on: an exploration of Reiki not as a complementary therapy, but as a lifestyle.

In a strange foreshadowing, I had titled the retreat 'Living the Light'. Seeing the light, sensing the light, takes a moment. But living it, bringing it into our daily routines, our families, our jobs, our passions, takes work. It is a pretty hard task.

Reiki as a complementary therapy is easy. Reiki as a lifestyle is tough. But I believe it can change the world.

It turned out to be the most intense and exhausting course I'd ever taught, but also incredibly rewarding.

In one exercise I asked everyone to connect with a person of their choice, not another participant but someone from their usual circle, not necessarily to send them Reiki, but to feel the connection between them. But there was a catch: I asked them not to choose someone they liked, but someone they particularly disliked. Somebody whose presence would make them uncomfortable, whether in a small, niggling way or to the extent that they wouldn't be able to bear being in the same room.

This is one the most challenging exercises I have tried, and a lot of people also clearly struggle with it. The challenge is that we may end up seeing the other person for what they are: another struggling human being. Another spiritual being. Just like us. No matter how much we dislike them, we are connected to the same Source. And we are connected to them. It may not be a welcome realisation.

On the last day of the retreat, I bumped into one of the participants in the souvenir shop. He was about to buy two identical souvenirs, and when I asked about it, he said, rather sheepishly, 'One is for me. The other one for the person I connected with in that exercise.'

For me, that was another moment of *satori*.

When the feedback arrived over the following weeks, I realised the transformation that this retreat had facilitated. And I started to wonder what would happen if more people – many, many more people – had access to Reiki. What would our world look like? What would the planet look like? What would society look like if lots of people had healing hands and lived every day with the awareness that they were part of a bigger picture, connected to something deeper – and to everyone else?

There was another experience that stayed with me. As the participants were from a variety of backgrounds, I hadn't wanted to accentuate the fact that the course was taking place in a

Christian monastery. I thought it would be interesting, though, to get a bit of an introduction to the monastery and monastic life, and towards the end of the retreat we were kindly invited to spend half an hour with a monk. He turned out to be a polite man in his thirties, and I'm sure I wasn't the only one wondering why he had chosen this unusual lifestyle.

After he had given us an overview of life in a Benedictine monastery, he actually addressed this question. He had known the monastery since childhood, had been a member of the famous boys' choir and had attended the boarding school. He had then lived in metropolitan Barcelona, but hadn't been able to find inner peace. Life was too busy, too overwhelming, too insecure.

Life at the monastery offered him the structure to find what he had been longing for: extended times of stillness; study and reflection; chanting and prayer; and working and living in a like-minded community.

Even years later, this monk's story often pops into my mind. Along with the question: is it really impossible to find peace in a normal life? Living a monastic life is certainly a way to find inner stillness and peace. And I am full of respect for such a decision. But aren't we given life in order to live it rather than retreat from it? If everyone joined a monastery, apart from obviously dying out as a species within a generation, how would we have all the fascinating experiences that shape us?

And if there are times when we struggle with life, aren't those the times in which we learn and develop even more?

Today, when I want to feel at peace, I place my hands on my chest and let Reiki flow. Even if times are challenging, nights sleepless and worries never-ending, I can still feel the peace that lies beyond everything. The problems have a beginning and an end, but the peace is eternal. But I wonder whether I would ever have found it without Reiki.

30.

Just an Idea

When people learn Reiki, they can: i) use it as a complementary therapy for themselves and those around them; ii) invite more harmony, balance, intuition and guidance into their lives; and iii) if they trace the energy of their 'healing hands' back, sense that they are connected to higher levels in the universe and experience a deep spiritual awakening.

The downside of Reiki is ... nothing. It's almost too good to be true, but there are absolutely no negatives. First, you don't have to commit to anything. Reiki is at your disposal whenever you need it, but it's up to you how and when you actually use it. Secondly, Reiki cannot do any harm. Not as a complementary therapy and certainly not as a spiritual development tool. And thirdly, you don't have to believe in anything – or renounce any established beliefs. Whether you follow a religion or a spiritual tradition or seek your answers in science or nature, Reiki can complement your individual path.

Given that there are no prerequisites or conditions, that it is extremely easy to learn and can provide extraordinary help, I feel there is a strong case for, well, *everybody* learning Reiki. And once we connect through Reiki with other people, we begin to comprehend that we are connected on a much deeper level as well: we are all from the same Source. This can definitely – and dramatically – change the way we interact with one another.

So, the more people learn Reiki, the better it is for them, for others and for the world. As Mikao Usui said in one of his few surviving quotes (from *Reiki Ryoho Hikkei*, a brochure published by the Reiki Gakkai for its 50th anniversary): '[It's about] walking [the] right path as a human being ... leading [a] peaceful and happy life, healing others and improving the happiness of others and ourselves.'

But how do you convince people to do what's good for them? Over the course of human history, most of the time this has failed. Or people have tried to impose systems that weren't really suitable for everybody. Or even had a detrimental effect. Or they have introduced new belief systems or societal structures with force, even violence.

Over the years, I've found that it is unhelpful to use even the gentlest persuasion in convincing others to try Reiki. They just feel pressured and react with resentment. Of course, we can (and should) make the offer, but then we need to wait for the person to choose for themselves and say: 'Yes, I really *would* like to try it out.'

So how do we inspire others to give Reiki a try?

I tend to find that often people start getting interested when they hear a personal story, for example they are sharing a problem with a friend and that person tells them how Reiki helped them with a similar problem. There are also many stories in books, on the internet and on social media about how people found Reiki and how it helped them.

But hearing or reading a story takes time, and in our fast-moving world people don't often stop to absorb and reflect. So, how else do you get their attention?

Over time, I've realised that my own attention is normally caught in two ways: either by an image or a sound. What always makes me stop is an image of change, a before-and-after. Of course, this is how Reiki is often experienced. But how do we capture it? We can't really take a picture of a person first looking sad then smiling. Not only would it look a bit cheap, but it would be impossible to prove that Reiki was the factor behind the smile.

Thinking about this one day, suddenly I had an idea. There was one exercise with the clearest before-and-after effect ever, and I had been promoting it for years! All that was needed was a measuring technique.

It had convinced scores of my Reiki students on their very first day of training, and would, if provable, mean that there was a novel scientific approach to evidencing Reiki. Because that had been the other problem in promoting Reiki: even if people listened to a story, they often wondered about the placebo effect. What about scientific proof?

The answer could be the *water test*.

The first time I tried it, I could hardly believe it! I filled two glasses with tap water, set the intention to connect to Reiki and then placed my hands around one of the glasses for a few minutes. The change in taste was mind-blowing!

I tried it again and again, then had friends and family testing it, and the vast majority could taste a difference. The Reiki-treated water tasted softer, more pleasant, more like natural spring water. Now, on every single Reiki 1 course I ask the students to try it out too, ideally on the very first evening when they arrive home –

though, of course, it's something that can only be done in countries where the tap water is safe for human consumption in the first place.

I once had a group of students who went to a pub after the completion of Reiki 1. They asked for two jugs of tap water at the bar, then gave Reiki to one and did the tasting. Again, the difference was mind-blowing.

If these results could be confirmed by a proper scientific test, I thought, it would be so much easier to convince people of the efficacy of Reiki. If it improved water, it would have a similar effect on our bodies, given that the vast majority of our body mass is water.

Finding a laboratory, however, was much easier said than done. I contacted several laboratories in the UK, none of which thought they had the right tools to make such fine measurements. I contacted several institutions in the United States, with the same result. Wasn't I meant to get this going?

Eventually, my sister suggested a small laboratory in Germany which specialised in analysing tap water to determine whether it was safe for babies to consume.

Again, they suggested that the measuring techniques available to them might not be suitable for the tests I was trying to do, as they only focused on a limited number of metals and pollutants present in the water. But they suggested the Hagalis Institute in Switzerland, which measured water quality with a novel technique and was renowned for being able to establish whether drinking water came from a natural source, like a mountain spring, or had been artificially cleansed and recycled. Their system was even used to certify bottled drinking water.

What really intrigued me was that as part of the process, images were taken under a microscope. The samples I saw showed fascinating differences between water types and qualities.

Of course I had been intrigued by the images of waster crystals taken by the Japanese researcher Masaru Emoto in the early 2000s. He had exposed water samples to a variety of influences, like spoken or written words of love or hatred, or even different kinds of music, and then frozen them and documented the crystals that were formed.

Negative influences, like words of hatred or ignorance, or even heavy metal music, led to ugly, distorted crystals, while positive influences led to beautiful, evenly shaped crystals. It was an amazingly simple way to confirm what psychologists and spiritual teachings had been suggesting for a long time: the world resonates with our input. Negative words or actions create even more negativity, while love brings positive change.

I got in contact the Hagalis Institute and a few days later boarded a flight to Zurich.

31.

Scientific Proof of Reiki

Once again, I was so nervous that I barely slept. The next morning I took an early cross-country train through the picturesque landscape of northern Switzerland. Unsurprisingly, it arrived right on time.

At the institute, I was greeted by the director, who showed me around the laboratory and detailed the process the water would be put through to establish its quality. He was careful to warn me not to have high expectations – they often had clients, from energy healers to inventors of new filtration methods, eagerly hoping for proof that their methods worked, but quite regularly the water didn't show many changes, if any at all.

Now it was Reiki's turn. Two sterilised glass bottles were filled with the local tap water. One was kept as a control; the other was placed on a desk for me to work on.

I sat down on a swivel chair, waited until I felt the connection to Reiki, then placed my hands around the bottle. Forty-five minutes later, the task was completed: I had focused my concentration on the flow of Reiki and felt the well-known sensation in my palms. Admittedly, it did feel a bit strange giving a Reiki treatment to a cold bottle of water for such an extended period, but it also felt excitingly right.

I was told that processing of the tests would take a few days and I should expect the results early the following week. In the event, however, the institute was so busy that it took three agonizing weeks for the detailed analysis to arrive.

As the institute certifies the quality of bottled drinking water for the German-speaking market, it uses a grading system that follows German school marks: one is the best, six the worst. The tap water control sample had a quality of 3.1 – average good-quality tap water, filtered and processed enough to be drinkable without any problems.

I flipped straight to the next page: Had the Reiki treatment made a difference?

It had.

After 45 minutes of Reiki, the quality had changed to 1.91, which meant it had moved into the 'spring water' range. The report called this a 'significant increase in quality'. In other words, Reiki must have stimulated the innate healing abilities of the water and reduced the detrimental effects of pollution and chemical cleansing. The sample had regained the power of *natural* water and its minerals had a high bioavailability.

There was more to come. Much more, actually. But let's pause for a moment, because that really was a sensational result, proving that Reiki had measurable physical effects, not just psychological ones. And the best thing about it: I had pictures! A clear before-and-after, with recognisable changes, even to the untrained eye.

In his accompanying letter, the institute's director actually congratulated me. He was truly surprised.

As the results were almost too good to be true, of course I had to make sure that the testing method met proper scientific standards. We cannot just accept a testing method without carefully examining its credentials. Two of the most obvious are repeatability and quantifiability: how often has the method been tried and have the results been consistent?

The accompanying report detailed the method, a number of publications were already in the public domain and the institute made other resources available to me so that the method could be properly scrutinised. So, before I give an overview of it, let me emphasise the most important fact: the method is backed by a body of consistent empirical data running into well over 10,000 tests. This alone meets established scientific standards.

The method itself is relatively simple: the water sample is divided into its solid and liquid components through distillation. While the remaining liquid is put to one side, the residue is cleared of any traces of organic materials through heat. After a few more steps of distillation and filtration, the minerals and water are recombined in a set ratio and then left to form liquid crystals. When the process is complete, one or several drops are placed on a glass tray and left to dry.

The crystallisation left on the glass is then analysed under a microscope. Every drop in a sample will end up showing the same basic structure.

The number of analyses completed by the laboratory has enabled them to build up a database of crystalline structures to determine the quality of the water. The determining factors are the length, clarity, quantity and distribution of the crystals on the glass tray. Occasionally, there is even a lack of significant crystallisation.

The most striking difference between crystalline structures lies in the angles formed. A 90-degree angle indicates that the water is – or used to be – polluted and, even possibly after a filtration and cleansing process, still carries all the hallmarks of this pollution. In this case, the structures are often cross-shaped. They almost looked like a graveyard to me.

Angles of 60 degrees, often in star or starfish shapes, are a clear indication that the water is natural and has not been tampered with. Sometimes slightly more organic shapes are produced, looking like leaves or flowers.

The finer, more detailed and more numerous the crystals, the better the quality of the water.

Among the samples analysed by the institute over the years have been some taken at various sections along rivers – the spring, further downstream, and after passing villages or urban developments that are likely to contribute sewage to the river. The crystallisation in the water samples has clearly showed the deterioration of the water.

With the ability to establish whether water is from a natural source, the institute has begun to be widely been used to certify that bottled water is of organic origin, rather than just filtered or chemically cleansed tap water.

The underlying idea, of course, is that natural water, filtered through layers of natural rock and sediment for sometimes thousands of years, with all the minerals and trace elements acquired along the way, is better for the human body. Just like organic food, it is not just supposed to have a higher concentration of nutrients, but to be closer to its natural state and potency. (Personally, I eat organic food as much as I can. I find it quite staggering how few restaurants offer organic ingredients, even now.)

You could say that, in essence, the institute measures something that for a long time wasn't considered measurable: life-force, *ki*, the stuff that you find in a fresh apple, but not as much in processed food.

We are, however, in tricky waters now: science. And I am certain that there will be differing opinions about this method of analysis. Let me therefore make it clear that my ultimate conclusions about Reiki are primarily based on my own experiences, both in my own life and with clients. There is also a degree of intuition and guidance involved. The water tests are supporting evidence, as it were, although extraordinary evidence, from a different angle.

I feel I should also add a word about science in general. Today, of course, *everything* is about science. But there is also, I find, a lot of misunderstanding about the term – and about what science is really able to deliver.

Following many discussions with scientists, I have learned there is actually a lot of disagreement. One theory is contradicted by another one, and, at least initially, new discoveries are rarely accepted across the board.

When I talk with Reiki sceptics, I often hear: 'Is there scientific proof?' or even: 'I believe in science.' There are actually two misunderstandings here: first, scientific proof is helpful, even greatly so – otherwise I wouldn't have looked for it and been so excited by the test results! – but it isn't everything. Many things indisputably exist, even though science hasn't been able to explain or measure them. Secondly, there are different scientific approaches, and science is far broader than simple physics or chemistry.

A few years ago, I met a distant cousin at a family gathering. Always top of his class, he is now an internationally respected pharmaceutical researcher, and very outspoken.

He walked over to me and asked, rather bluntly, without any small talk beforehand, 'So, Torsten, can you explain to me what this Reiki stuff that you're doing actually is?'

I wasn't quite sure how to meet the level of explanation I thought would be acceptable to him and tried to sound as 'scientific' as I could. But as soon as I mentioned the words 'quantum physics', he rather rudely interrupted me, saying, 'I hate it when people talk about something they don't understand!'

Being very aware of the famous quote by Nobel Prize-winning physicist Richard Feynman, 'I think I can safely say that nobody understands quantum mechanics,' I hadn't even been pretending to understand it, merely to illustrate the idea that everything is connected.

As this had obviously failed, I took a deep breath and tried a different tack: 'I am so pleased that you are here with your girlfriend tonight!'

He was in fact introducing her to the family.

'How would you describe what attracted you to her?' I asked. 'Would you maybe say that you are, somehow, "in love"? How would you measure that?'

After his initial surprise, he started smiling and said, 'Good answer. I can accept that.'

And so he should. Despite the difficulties measuring it, I suppose it would be highly unscientific to deny the existence of love.

Science isn't just about data either – it's about the method applied to collect them. This "scientific model" is applied in three steps:

1. We observe something and wonder what it is all about. We try to understand it better and come to a conclusion, for example: 'When x, y, z does this, then a, b, c seems to be the result.' This is our starting hypothesis. With Reiki, it would be: 'I give somebody a Reiki treatment and, very broadly speaking, there is a noticeable positive effect.'

2. Then we come up with a strategy to evaluate this hypothesis: for example, we give Reiki treatments to a number of people and record the results. (The more people involved, the higher the validity of the results.)

3. Open-mindedly, we analyse the collected data and see whether they support our original hypothesis or not. We

196

may get neither a confirmation nor a contradiction of our hypothesis, but learn something completely new.

The deeper we go into a subject, the narrower the hypothesis can be, and the more precise the understanding gained, for example: what is the starting condition; what are the influencing factors; what is the physical effect; what is the psychological effect?

Basically, this is science: trial and error, all neatly recorded and analysed. Then we base the next hypothesis and set of tests on what we have learned so far. The more creative we are with our hypotheses, and the more open-minded when analysing the outcome of the tests, the more science can be advanced.

Data, though, aren't always completely clear and can be interpreted in different ways. Occasionally, scientists seem more at war with one another than on the same mission of understanding the universe. And a big part of science, of course, is merely hypothetical. It rests on logic rather than tests in a laboratory, and is therefore much more difficult to evaluate. Stephen Hawking was famous for following his amazingly logical theories, but still didn't always get it right. For over 35 years, he defended his theory that black holes ate energy and that once it got in one, it was lost. This entirely contradicted other theories that energy simply mutated and could never be lost. Eventually, Hawking changed his mind and accepted that energy didn't get lost in a black hole, only condensed. He used the term *singularity* and came to a conclusion that I am paraphrasing here: 'Everything starts in singularity, then expands and divides into a myriad of energetic vibrations, resulting in the complexity of the universe, and, one day, ends up in dense singularity again. Individuality, then, is lost, but the memory of the experiences remains.'

I don't think there is a much better way to describe eternity.

For now, though, I just want to put the discoveries about Reiki into perspective. There isn't science on one side and Reiki on the other. Science is always developing, and slowly catching up with the reality of Reiki.

Let me finish this chapter with one more thought: the scientific model – hypothesis, collection of data, analysis – can be applied to any setting. Science isn't always rocket science. It can include not just chemistry, physics and mathematics, but also 'soft' sciences like sociology, education and comparative religious studies. Or political science, in which I obtained my master's degree.

The key to maintaining academic standards is objectivity. It was therefore majorly helpful that the Hagalis Institute had no interest in a specific outcome of my tests. The fee wasn't dependent on certain results.

Personally, of course, I was thrilled with the results we obtained … and soon I would be back for more.

32.

Proof, Round Two

As soon as the effect of Reiki had been confirmed, my imagination went into overdrive: what if a test could also show the effect of the Reiki *symbols*? Could this be a way of establishing the different vibrational levels that Reiki worked on?

The biggest consideration was the rather high cost involved, but if my hopes were realised, it would be well worth it, so once again I took out a loan and booked a flight.

This time, I had arranged to be in the laboratory for an entire day. I was placed in the same room as before, literally at the same desk, and, after warning the laboratory staff that they might hear some strange noises, I got to work straight away. Sterilised bottles were again filled with tap water, only several more this time, as I had planned a whole range of tests.

Again, one bottle was set side as a control, then the others were brought in one by one. I wanted the treatments to be similar to an average professional Reiki treatment and allowed one hour for each.

In the first treatment, I focused on 'general Reiki', with no additions and no symbols, and was pleased that I managed to keep mental images of the symbols entirely at bay. This was Reiki as a Reiki 1 student would have used it, although I couldn't rule out the possibility that my years of using Reiki might result in a stronger connection than one made straight after a first attunement.

In the second treatment, I took a fresh sample and focused on the Power Symbol: I drew it in the air, then above the bottle, I visualised it, drew it on my palms and drew it directly on the bottle. Just as in a normal treatment, from time to time I moved my hands, placing them on different parts of the bottle, sometimes moving them away and sometimes just holding the bottle. I regularly repeated the symbol's mantra, *Cho Ku Rei*, and chanted the *kotodama*, connecting to Reiki by using sound. (More on this later.)

Concentrating on just one symbol at a time worked surprisingly well. The next was the Harmony Symbol. Again, I took a fresh water sample, then drew the symbol, repeated the mantra, *Sei Heki*, and chanted the *kotodama*.

Then came the Connection Symbol, and after that, to get the whole picture, I gave a final treatment using the Master Symbol. And we kept one further untreated bottle in storage so that I could send Reiki to it from a distance at a later stage.

I gave three treatments in the morning, then went for lunch. When I returned, I had a surprise: the director couldn't wait to share the first test results!

While waiting for the crystallisation to take place, the laboratory staff had carried out another form of analysis: measuring the concentration of negative ions. This simple test indicates whether physical healing is taking place.

The director said, 'Mr Lange, we made a really interesting discovery: the first new test, the one you labelled "Power", showed a significant increase in negative ions. From that we conclude that it was meant to promote physical healing. The next example, though, the one that you labelled "Harmony", had a very different result: there was no increase at all! We've got the feeling that it is used for something else, not physical healing.'

I was stunned. This was like hitting the jackpot! Never in my wildest dreams could I have predicted that the differences would be that obvious.

When all the tests were completed, I went for a very long walk to digest the results so far. If they were an indication of what was to come, it would be nothing short of extraordinary. I was sure that in some way it would have an impact on the world.

It was a particularly beautiful summer's day, and I remember sitting in a lakeside restaurant phoning everybody I could get hold of – my sister, my friends and of course Mum – to tell them about the results we had obtained. There was no way I could keep them to myself!

The following weeks seemed to be some of the slowest of my life. Then one day there were three emails with lots of attachments. And a clarity I had never expected.

I had taken a few days off and was actually sitting on the beach when the first email came through on my phone. With limited mobile coverage, it took ages to download the attachments and I clearly remember how difficult it was to zoom in on the images.

When I finally managed it, I turned to my rather surprised neighbour and said, 'This can change the world!'

I just couldn't help myself. I was looking at a visual representation of the different levels of the universe.

For this series of tests, I had asked for additional images of each sample to get a better visual idea of what was happening. They were taken at different magnifications, with the highest showing the very fine details of the crystallisation and the smaller ones showing the entire water sample. These were the most fascinating, as the distribution of the crystals turned out to be key.

In the test using the Power Symbol, there were the starfish-like crystals you would find in good-quality spring water. Looking at the entire sample, they were remarkably evenly distributed from the edge to the centre. In other words, the energy had gone into every part of the water, just as you would want in physical healing, which is the intention behind the symbol.

With the Harmony Symbol, the crystals looked slightly more delicate. And interestingly, there was nothing in the centre of the sample – all the crystals were grouped around the edge, as if they were pointing outwards, towards something else. This wasn't about physicality; it was about going beyond it.

The most striking images, though, were from the Connection Symbol. Not only were the crystals larger, they had actually started to touch one another. They were growing towards one another, connecting.

Finally, the Master Symbol showed all of the above in one image, on every level at once.

I looked at the pictures again and again and again. There was more here. This wasn't just proof of healing, it was proof of the different vibrational levels of the universe.

33.

The Science within Reiki

Staring at the images, I realised that after all these years, I had still been looking in the wrong direction. This wasn't about proof of Reiki's efficacy as a complementary therapy, which had already been detailed in both clinical trials and case studies all around the world, but what Reiki could tell us about the structure of the universe. I wasn't looking at scientific proof *of* Reiki but the science *within* Reiki.

Reiki, really, is a way to understand the different vibrational levels of the universe and how we are connected to them.

The Reiki symbols are connected to three levels of existence: the Power Symbol is connected to the level of *form*; the Harmony Symbol is connected to the level of *spirit;* and the Connection Symbol is connected to what you might call a level or simply an awareness of *oneness* or the interconnectedness of everything. But – and this is a big but – this isn't just a way to *understand* the universe. It isn't even just a way to feel a *connection* with these different vibrational levels. We are *already* connected to every level of the universe. So, Reiki is a way of *realisation*. Or, to use the famous philosophical term, *self-realisation*.

The Reiki symbols also correspond to the major energy centres in our bodies, the *Tanden* points. Once we start to understand this, we also begin to understand that we're not just random figures within a universe, we're intrinsically linked to it. And this allows us to use Reiki in even more empowering ways.

You could say that the universe is the macrocosm and we are the microcosm, or that the universe is a reflection of us and we are a reflection of the universe. The two cannot be separated, no matter how separate we sometimes feel.

To illustrate this, let me take a moment to go a little deeper into the centuries-old concept behind the *Tanden*. While few people have heard of the *Tanden* (*Dantien* in Chinese, sometimes also called the three diamonds), most are familiar with the chakra system. The chakras are, basically, energy centres, junctions, or points of connection in our subtle energy system and are linked to the ancient Eastern understanding that the human body is made up of subtle energetic vibrations. These vibrations sustain life.

Many complementary therapies, from acupuncture to reflexology, are based on this understanding. When we give Reiki treatments, we often feel particular sensations over the chakras, and this can tell us more about the nature of the problems or blockages the person is experiencing.

It's all the more surprising then that the chakra system wasn't general knowledge in Japan at the time of Mikao Usui. The focus then was on only three main energy centres. But let me add that there is absolutely no contradiction between the two systems. After all, truth may be seen from different angles, but will remain the same.

The *Tanden* system groups the chakras around three main focal points: the naval chakra (summing up the lower chakras), the brow chakra (for the upper chakras), and the heart chakra (as the very centre, but closely connected to the sacral and throat chakras).

The Lower Tanden – Hara, the Level of Form

We often find the word *hara* in Japanese culture, probably most famously as part of the word *hara-kiri*, a form of committing suicide by jumping onto a sword or knife that penetrates the *hara*. The understanding is that the *hara* is the energy centre of the physical body, the centre of the individual life-force. It is located about an inch below the navel. Physical strength builds up from this point. Sumo-wrestlers, for instance, focus on it.

In Mikao Usui's system of Reiki, this energy centre is closely connected with the Power Symbol, as it relates to all aspects of physicality, from bodily functions, health and strength to being grounded, focused and in the here and now. We experience an incarnation in a physical body, so it's important that it works. Unlike quite a few spiritual traditions, Reiki does not set aside normal life. If anything, it helps us to make the most of it.

I would say it is fair to assume that the water test showed that nature's innate self-healing abilities are stimulated through Reiki. If additional help is needed, like surgery or medication, Reiki can help with side-effects and healing.

The Power Symbol images showed the crystallisation going right through the water sample, deep into the physical structure. And this is what the mantra that accompanies the Power Symbol also illustrates: *Cho Ku Rei* means 'cutting action of a sword', as in clearing blockages and directing healing power to the areas of need. Furthermore, the symbol includes a spiral, which, when drawn, leads straight to the centre of the physical problem.

So, Reiki can help with physical problems. That's official. But let's take a step back: why do we have problems in the first place? Why do we *need* help?

Being in a body can be a blessing or a challenge, depending on how well the body performs. We experience individuality, but also separation. We often identify with our physical shape and abilities, which can undermine our confidence. And our body can only be in one physical place at a time, which often leads us to wish we were somewhere else.

Most people accept this state as normal, rather than as an artificial restriction for a limited period only. But it *is* a restriction – and it is for a limited period. This highlights the key feature of life on the level of form: it has a beginning and an end. Experiencing the end of an individual life on Earth feels painful and sad, but it is also the end of the many limitations that come with an incarnation. An incarnation allows us to experience what it is like to be a part, but not complete.

But amazingly, the other symbols allow us to go beyond this format even while we are still in a body.

The Upper Tanden – *the Level of Spirit*

I find it surprising how little information is in the public domain about the other two *Tanden*. The *hara* is mentioned everywhere, from martial arts instructions to meditation manuals, but the others are almost secret. I assume that it is left to individual students to discover them, which would be a typical way of

207

teaching in ancient Eastern traditions. But it also means that the majority of people today miss out on discovering these different vibrational levels. Are they meant to be kept in the three-dimensional experience? Is higher awareness only for a small elite?

Mikao Usui wanted the system of Reiki to be accessible to everyone. He therefore created symbols for people to access the higher-vibrational levels instantly. In this way, his system is different from any other Eastern esoteric tradition. It is remarkable how much this aspect has been overlooked. Mikao Usui was a true rebel who broke with established cultural customs.

The opening of the upper *Tanden* used to be associated with deep meditation techniques and years of practice. After Reiki attunements, though, many students start feeling a sensation between their eyebrows straight away. It can feel like a gentle migraine and is a sign that something is happening in the region of the brow chakra.

Actually located just above the midpoint between the eyebrows, this energy centre is often called the 'third eye', as it represents the understanding that there is more to see than our physical eyes are capable of: a reality that is less dense but just as important as the physical one.

The Harmony Symbol opens us up to this higher-vibrational level and so brings more harmony and balance into our everyday lives and helps us to access intuition and guidance.

I tend to find that the key word for this vibrational level, 'spiritual', is often either disliked or misunderstood. I recently learned that a leading Reiki organisation had discussed dropping it entirely from its website, as it might put off more scientifically minded people. As if they don't have a soul too! The word 'spiritual' is essential for an understanding of how Reiki works, as it refers to the fact that the three-dimensional world isn't all that exists and there is a higher-vibrational level too. It has no shape or location and it isn't possible to measure it, but it is possible to experience it. It is a level of many different layers. It is where we, as individual souls, come from and return to. It is where we rest and recuperate between incarnations. So, the word 'spiritual' is really just the recognition that our physical existence has a beginning and an end, but our individual soul carries on after death.

We have thoughts, we have ideas, we have a mind, we have mental challenges, we have emotions – all these are higher vibrations. You could say they exist between the three-dimensional and higher levels, connected to our individual physical existence, but beyond the density of form.

We can also access non-physical guidance, although we often don't trust it, at least initially. In Reiki, it often starts with a feeling of where to place our hands. We want to treat a knee, for instance, and somehow feel drawn to another area of the body like the ankles or hips. More often than not, the feedback later explains why our intuition was right. We may also get an idea of the root cause of the problem our client is experiencing.

The fashionable word 'flow' comes in here too, meaning that we are tapping into the higher wisdom and inspiration that our soul carries. Indeed, using the Harmony Symbol strengthens this connection, up to the point where we may get messages from beings on the 'other side': spirit guides, loved ones who have passed away and angelic beings. The experiences laid out in this book are a clear illustration of this.

Fascinatingly, the images from the Harmony Symbol water analysis illustrate this perfectly: the crystal shapes moving to the edges, as if they want to reach out to another dimension and don't solely identify with the physical level.

The Harmony Symbol was inspired by the symbol for Amida Nyorai, the Buddhist 'deity' whose statue I encountered on Mt Kurama. Although the Harmony Symbol was designed exclusively for Reiki, ensuring that it wasn't connected to any religion, the two symbols share the same basic elements and point to the same meaning: access to higher vibrations, help, guidance and acceptance – a direct connection to the spiritual realm.

The targets of this symbol are the obstacles in our minds – the mistaken beliefs, the feelings of being lost or singled out. The accompanying mantra puts it very clearly: *Sei Heki* means 'bad habit' and the symbol is designed to replace it. It doesn't target what most people classify as bad habits, though, like eating habits, laziness or the contemporary use of the word in Japan, which implies kinky practices or sexual fantasies, but the underlying bad habit of not recognizing that there is much more to us than the restrictions of physicality. We are spiritual beings and therefore powerful enough to overcome the negativity, the sadness, the frustration, the depression, the anger and the addictions that are all part of our three-dimensional existence. On the higher levels, they simply dissolve.

So, the idea behind the Harmony Symbol's mantra is similar to the Power Symbol's mantra: on the level of form, the mantra is about cutting open the problem and letting Reiki inside; on the level of spirit, it is about cutting away the habits that hold us back. There is no judgement, only help.

Drawing the symbol is a journey of accessing this: we start by going round sharp angles, navigating through the challenges of our earthly experience, then move into the softer, smoother, gentler vibrations symbolised by round strokes.

We aren't just replacing bad habits, we're moving beyond them. Once we do that, once we feel the connection to the higher levels, we automatically know we are safe, we are loved and we are guided.

On the first ever Western Reiki Master certificate, issued in 1938 for Hawayo Takata by Mikao Usui's Master student Chujiro Hayashi, Reiki was described as 'a system of natural, drugless healing'. Of course, behind this rather lovely terminology was the understanding that Reiki does not use any medication, just energy. But, looking at the trend of seeking spiritual experiences by taking drugs, it can also be applied here: the psychic experiences we get through Reiki don't need any drugs either. Seeing colours, symbols and scenes and having a sudden insight into a problem are related to the use of this vibrational level.

The Middle Tanden – Oneness

The middle or central *Tanden* is located at the heart. It is, as the water test shows, the most powerful. But we don't need the water test to know that love is a very powerful force. And that is what this symbol is all about.

Under the microscope, the crystallisation showed large and refined starfish shapes literally trying to connect with each other

211

– to touch. Interestingly, it led to an even bigger leap in the quality of the water. Connection can also lead to a quantum leap in the quality of our lives.

The heart is the place where we feel connection, and from where we establish a close bond with somebody else. Often, this is the bond of romantic love, or love for friends and family. It is all about a *special* connection, sometimes even an exclusive one – after all, we don't give or open our heart to everybody. Having said that, though, even though we feel more attracted to some people than others (and then often only for a certain period), we already have a deep connection to *everyone*. Romantic love and family love just show us what we are capable of. With most people, we don't even feel the connection. But it is still there.

The Connection Symbol reminds us of that connection and helps us to utilise it: by using the symbol, we can connect with anybody, anywhere in the world, and give them a Reiki treatment. We can connect to situations and places too, and often get such extraordinary insights that even the least intuitive of us feels psychic. And of course this symbol enabled me to give distant attunements to my online students, who often told me that they felt as if I was standing right next to them.

Drawing the symbol makes seemingly individual words inseparable, because this isn't really a symbol, but a sentence put together in *kanji*, the Japanese logographic characters, and written in such a way that the end of one word forms the beginning of the next and they share the same strokes. As a result, it can be read and understood, but the words can't be taken apart anymore – that would make them incomplete and meaningless. Just as we often feel incomplete and that our life is meaningless when we feel on our own.

The sequence of words in the symbol is its mantra, *Hon Sha Ze Sho Nen*, which can be translated as 'My original being is a correct thought.' I am not a seemingly lost individual; I am always connected to the universe. And to every other being within it.

This concept isn't always easy to apply in everyday life! But when we do apply it, extraordinary things can happen: we can overcome division and misunderstandings, and our lives can be completely transformed.

Distance is artificial, created for a temporary experience only. And so is time. The Connection Symbol is based on the realisation that everything is interconnected – cutting through time and space.

Rei *and* Ki

It has become more and more obvious to me how close the connection between the *Tanden* and the three Reiki symbols really is. This is even anchored in the word *Reiki*.

At the time of Mikao Usui, there was the idea that there were seven vibrational levels in the universe. The further away they were from the Source, the denser and slower they became, with the solidity of physical reality forming the outermost level. Reiki was the name of the highest vibration – you could say the one where Creator and creation came together. That's why some people call it 'Source energy'. It was seen as the gateway between the changeable, impermanent structure of the created universe and the eternal core – pure light.

When we look at the *kanji* of Reiki in ancient Japanese, this becomes even clearer. The word *Reiki* consists of two parts, *Rei* and *Ki*. *Ki* is the much better known, being the same as *prana* in yogic traditions, or *chi* in *tai chi* or *chi gong*. It describes the life-force: higher-vibrational energy without which we wouldn't function or even be alive. This energy needs to flow freely – when it is blocked, illness occurs.

Ki is very much connected to our bodily existence: the asterix in the *kanji* stands for the word *kome*, a grain of rice – a physical object, food, the basis of life on Earth. The strokes around it, *kigamae* in Japanese, point to the fact that there is also higher energy present. It can be translated as 'ether' and refers to what today is often called the biofield.

Of course, over time blockages build up, and it often becomes difficult to follow the flow of life. We feel stuck in our bodily existence and need help. This is when the element of *Rei* comes in.

The word *Rei* itself is made up of three elements: *ame*, *utsuwa* and *miko*. The top part looks like rain, and that is exactly what *ame* means. There is a cover, firmament or sky, from which rain is falling. Help is coming from a higher level in the form of higher-vibrational energy, healing, guidance and practical change. We are nourished and our life-force energy can flourish again.

In order to bring the help down, though, we need to ask for it. And this is an important aspect: after all, we have free will. Entering the restrictions of physicality was our own choice. Accessing higher-vibrational energy, therefore, is a decision that we need to make too. Before we can do this, however, we need to know that it exists! Being aware that there is a deeper reality and knowing how to access it require wisdom. The word *miko* represents this: it can be translated as 'wise person', 'priestess' or 'shaman'.

In between these two aspects we find an interesting third one: the connection to our bodies, our lives and the concept of the different levels. The three boxes stand for the word *utsuwa*, meaning 'container' or 'mouth'. They represent the three *Tanden* – the navel, heart and brow chakras, the levels of form, interconnectedness and spirit.

More and more, I realised that this was an aspect that wasn't really covered by normal Reiki courses. But imagine using Reiki and its symbols to focus on these three energy centres, while at the same time deepening our awareness of these aspects of our existence. We would become much more complete.

Within weeks, I had written a new training programme to deepen our understanding of this science *within* Reiki. I called it 'ReikiScience'. The focus was on more detailed information about the Reiki symbols and new techniques to open our *Tanden*.

The first live course in London was mainly booked by Reiki Masters, and the feedback exceeded all my expectations: it had deepened not just their understanding but also their experience of Reiki. The most moving comment came from a student who said she just didn't want the course to end.

Only one part turned out to be different from what I had planned: the attunement. It provided a breakthrough I had never anticipated in my wildest dreams.

34.

Magenta

I had felt drawn to offering an attunement with this course, both in the live and the online versions, with the idea of focusing on the actual *Tanden* points rather than the symbols themselves. When I started to prepare myself energetically for it, I suddenly saw something new: a deep, intense pink. Magenta.

Colours are a way of translating energy into a visual experience, and, like many Reiki practitioners, I often saw them – most of the time just purple, the colour associated with the crown chakra and spiritual opening, sometimes one or two colours, sometimes an entire rainbow. But this was very different.

Years before, I had heard that magenta was the colour of oneness, but not really understood why. Now I did. Seeing magenta was the result of a powerful opening of the heart. And really, Reiki was all about the heart. All about love.

Every time I have given 'ReikiScience' attunements since, I have felt bathed in magenta – and in love. Many students have had similar experiences. Some have told me they felt love for the entire day, others that they felt their heart opening. Even established Reiki Masters have commented that this was a new level of attunement unlike any they'd had before.

I started to realise that I had talked about the different levels in the universe without really accepting them. Of course, there was a level of form, and clearly something higher, a level of spirit. But oneness wasn't really a level for me, but some kind of awareness. It turned out that this was a misconception.

Looking back at when I was introduced to the *Tanden*, I realised how much of a difference terminology could make. I had loved the idea that the Power Symbol was connected to *Earth* energy, as it was put to me then. And I still think this isn't really too far away from the idea of the level of form. It's about the planet, about our physical experience in an incarnation. But it gets much more difficult with the Harmony Symbol, which, I was told, was about *heaven* energy. 'Bringing energy from heaven into the here and now – what a wonderful idea!' was my amazed reaction. Wow, getting an idea of what paradise was like…

Well, this turned out to not be entirely the case.

The level of spirit is still … a level. Though of far finer density than the level of form, it is a level where there are still individual beings. Families recognize each other there and friends and lovers regroup. When we raise our vibrations on the level of form, as in the practice of Reiki, and connect with people on the spirit level, they still appear to have individual identities and memories, and huge fondness and love for the people they have been with in previous lives. And it is on this level that we prepare for our next incarnation, our next learning experience, though it seems that learning continues on this level too.

We like to think of this level as heaven, especially when we are experiencing hell here, on the level of form. But the spirit world is also only a transitional experience, if a revelatory one. While its lower-vibrational levels are still quite connected to the Earth and earthly experiences, the higher ones are more universal and allow us to eventually move *between* universes. Then the incredible vastness of creation becomes more obvious to us, as does the potential of Reiki, universal energy.

The *original* idea of heaven, though, is based on eternity, not on transition. Heaven, therefore, is beyond both of these levels.

And we don't have to wait to catch at least a glimpse of it. Heaven can be right here, right now.

Heaven is when we overcome separation. When we go beyond the experience of levels and open up to oneness and love.

Romantic love, love for children and closeness to family and friends are steps towards this. But they are still conditional – on mutual (or sometimes not so mutual) attraction, on the children being *our* children, or on being on the same *wavelength*. The connections can remain over several incarnations, forming something like a soul family. But they are still only transitional.

Oneness, on the other hand, means we are connected to everyone. *Every single one.* Until we can feel unconditional love for every single person in the universe, we are not in heaven.

Heaven is the opposite of individuality, of ego. The complete opposite. Is it therefore impossible to reach?

It isn't. Because it is already here. Whether we look at quantum physics or ancient spiritual teachings, we find the interconnectedness of all beings as the basic set-up of the universe.

We just need to rediscover it. And we can do it through Reiki.

35.

Kotodama –
a New Way to Access Higher Powers

Our 'healing hands', special breathing exercises and intuitive sensing of energy can all take us to the awareness of oneness. But there are two more ways, which I feel are particularly relevant at present. The first is *kotodama*, a way of connecting to Reiki by using sound.

As new as it may be to most people's Reiki practice, this is ancient wisdom in Japan. The premise behind it is that every word has a soul and by saying a word out loud, we are tapping into its essence and sharing its vibrations with others.

This is a timely reminder to choose our words carefully. Every word we say has an effect.

Of course, the Reiki symbols are also connected to words through their mantras. Saying them, or even better repeating them, has a noticeable effect. But some Japanese *kotodama* traditions go even further and reduce a word to its bare essentials, primarily the vowels, which appears to multiply its energetic resonance.

A few decades ago, this concept was applied to the mantras of the Reiki symbols, with extraordinary success. Just by chanting a string of vowels, it is possible to really feel the energetic vibrations that the Reiki symbols open us up to. Initially known to only a relatively small number of Reiki practitioners, in recent years this has gained in popularity and is now used in some Reiki workshops.

For many years, I had my Reiki 2 and Master students chant the *kotodama* together and they found it a powerful experience. Some even continued to use the chants as meditations at home.

I included them in my first live 'ReikiScience' training, as I wanted to explore all aspects of the symbols more deeply, and had my students chant for longer periods. The room was brimming with energy and it seemed to resonate deep within, which gave me an idea…

To my knowledge, the *kotodama* hadn't been tried out in actual Reiki treatments. They were normally chanted by practitioners for their own use, but not shared with people who weren't already attuned to Reiki. If it had an effect on them as well, it would be a completely novel way to give Reiki treatments. And could reach so many more people!

Always looking for further research opportunities, a few months after the first water tests I found an institute working with a very similar system. It was based in Germany, and I arranged to go there, primarily to repeat the initial tests and check whether the results were similar.

They did confirm the original findings. But while I was there, I suddenly had the idea of trying out something new. I bought two bottles of spring water, put one aside as a control and placed the other next to my mobile on the table in my hotel room.

As I had a recording of myself chanting the *kotodama* for the Power Symbol on my phone, I let it play while I left the room for 30 minutes. I didn't want my presence to interfere with the result, otherwise it would have been unclear whether any effect was created by the recording or the energy I might subconsciously have added.

Then I took both bottles straight to the laboratory.

Once again I was in for a surprise: When I got the results a few weeks later, the crystallisation of the spring water turned out to be much better structured after being exposed to the *kotodama*. The water quality had significantly improved. And this was after being exposed to merely a *recording* of the *kotodama*!

In other words, the sound acted as a portal to access Reiki without the presence of a practitioner. In future, it would be possible to have Reiki treatments simply by listening to such recordings!

I was probably as shocked as I was excited: did this mean the end of the need for Reiki practitioners?

It didn't. Further research showed that hands-on healing had a stronger effect. But the sound recordings could open doors in a myriad of ways. They could be used as a background when giving Reiki treatments, played in hospitals, or listened to on a regular basis or over prolonged periods. They could even be played at a low volume while people were sleeping. After all, regularity and time are important factors in Reiki treatments.

I subsequently made recordings of all the *kotodama*, some on their own, some interchanging with music, and built a short course around it that I called 'The Reiki Sound Healing Clinic'.

When covid-19 made its devastating way around the world and, inexplicably, most complementary therapists were banned from working in hospitals (showing a remarkable lack of understanding of complementary therapy's role in supporting the immune system), I decided to give the sound healing clinic away for free.

In the end, several thousand people signed up and the feedback confirmed the laboratory findings. It ranged from better sleep, improved sciatica, greater balance and a reduction in stress all the way to seeing colours and having out-of-body experiences. All purely through listening to a recording.

I'm sure that there will be many ways to utilise this in the future.

36.

A Journey to Love – the Reiki Principles

The second and very different way to bring Reiki into daily life is to apply the Reiki principles – something I initially strongly resisted. When I heard them for the first time, I thought they were a kind of aberration. They really didn't fit in with my understanding of Reiki. Reiki was a practice, the principles were theory. They sounded conservative, demanding and not at all in line with my idea of Reiki. It certainly didn't help that when I first came across them, I wasn't even given the original version.

I was therefore all the more surprised to see that on Mikao Usui's memorial stone they were almost centre-stage. I have quoted them already, but will repeat them here:

> *First it reads, 'Just for today, do not be angry,'*
>
> *secondly it reads, 'Do not worry,'*
>
> *thirdly it reads, 'Be thankful,'*
>
> *fourthly it reads, 'Work with diligence,'*
>
> *fifthly it reads, 'Be kind to others.'*

Over the years, I got closer to them. In fact, my retreat in Montserrat was structured around them. But even then, I felt I hadn't really found the key to them.

For a long time, I tried to apply intellectual understanding to them. And that made sense: we are happier when we aren't angry; we can trust more deeply when we aren't worried; it entirely changes our perception when we look for the positives and what we can be grateful for. Working with diligence was, for a long time, the most difficult to understand, but I accepted that the more we lived in the present moment and did what circumstances demanded of us, and did that with the best intentions, it would help us and everybody else. And being kind to others was of course just the right thing to do.

But step by step, I realised that it wasn't really necessary to understand these principles intellectually. Simply by reciting them and letting them sink in, we would find them popping up at the right moment and setting us on a journey – a journey of raising our energetic vibration.

Anger and worry are the opposite of raised vibrations. They hold us back. They are exclusively connected to the level of form, to daily survival, to identification with the physical body. The more we look beyond the physical, the more we feel a connection to something beyond it, the less we *need* anger, because we see that everything is an experience. And if we don't like the experience, possibly because what's going on isn't ethically acceptable, then anger doesn't get us any further. We need to make a change ourselves.

Worry keeps us back, too. And yet it is a very, very normal human emotion, which I'm nowhere near free of. To a large degree, this book has been written during the covid crisis. My Reiki Academy has been closed for more than a year and I've had almost no income. It has been a time of great uncertainty and of course I've been very worried. How could I not have been? The whole world has been! But every time I realised that my actions were being driven by fear rather than trust, I became stronger. I eventually decided, albeit reluctantly, that worry wouldn't get me anywhere.

Gratitude, on the other hand, changes everything. I'd never realised just how powerful this simple tool could be! As soon as we not only accept things as they are but realise how grateful we can be for these experiences, the energy completely shifts. Within us and around us. So often now I catch myself taking things for granted – anything from food to the weather to my home. And the people around me! I rarely sit down and say thank you for the sunshine, thank you for the sandwich, thank you for the bus taking me from A to Z, or thank you for the amazing conversation I just had with someone. But when I do, I feel a huge shift.

And that is what this principle is all about. It's about shift, it's about change. It's about stepping up a gear and raising our vibrations from the ones that keep us back – anger and worry – then accelerating through gratitude and realising, 'I'm here for a reason. And I'm stepping into my power.'

Diligence means just this, stepping into our power as a spiritual being and doing what is right.

There are various ways to translate the ancient Japanese wording. 'Diligence' is one, 'honesty' another – seeing things as they are and realising that they are level of form, they're three-dimensional. And that it is up to us to do the right thing and bring change.

Another word for this is 'decency'. Old-fashioned maybe, but very needed. If in every situation we started thinking, 'What's the decent thing to do? What's the right thing to do? Not the one that brings me the greatest praise and success, or the least difficult path, but the right thing, even if that's a challenge. Now that I understand who I am – a spiritual being – and that I have support, I can step in and *do* something.'

And finally, *being kind to others*. Which really is a contradiction in terms, because there are no others. So, it's about realising that we are all one and applying this in our daily lives. Once we treat others as equals, once we treat them as brothers and sisters, once we treat them as spiritual beings, as divine beings, then we have arrived.

The Reiki principles really are a journey from feeling lost in anger and worry to embracing love as the only truth and the greatest force in the universe. They are designed as a journey of raising our vibration. Another way of living Reiki.

There is no judgement, just encouragement. That's why the principles start with the words 'just for today'. Just give it a go. If, by the end of the day, you find that it hasn't always worked, just remember that the whole idea behind an incarnation is to learn from your mistakes. So, try again tomorrow. And the next day.

I always took these principles as a tool for personal development. But what if they could be rules for society? What if a whole country were to use them as the basis for living together? Or the whole world?

Mikao Usui is quoted as saying, 'In modern times, we have to live together. That will be the basis of happiness...'

Now, there's a thought…

37.

Reiki for the 21st Century

The longer I worked on this book, the more I became aware of Mikao Usui's guidance. As I wrote, he became an almost constant presence, helping me to translate my experiences into a way for us all to expand our understanding of Reiki. I often felt a nudge to stop and was then made aware that I should reword what I had just written, or move in a slightly different direction. Often, this ended in full – and sometimes really entertaining – conversations. Mikao Usui has an amazing sense of humour.

At one point, a few days passed without him stepping into my writing process, so I started to wonder if he had disappeared. Immediately there he was at my side again, telling me that he hadn't been needed, as he completely agreed with what I had been working on. 'Don't worry, I'm not letting you write what I don't agree with,' he said with a big smile.

The outline of the book had been pretty clear when I started to write; only the final chapter had been undefined. I had a rough idea that it would be about our individual connection to the universe and how to bring this awareness into everyday life, but the closer I got to it, the less sure I was about the details. When my copy-editor emailed out of the blue to tell me that a few weeks later she would have a free slot to work on the book, I suddenly felt under a lot of pressure. Which turned out to be a good thing: within five days, I had completed the first part; a week later, the second. But I was getting more and more nervous about the third, and about the conclusion.

Then Mikao Usui's gentle voice came again: 'Don't worry, just write. Once you are there, there will be a surprise for you. Don't worry about how to finish it now, it will come. And it will be different from what you think.'

Typically, I immediately began to wonder what the surprise might be. I came up with a whole range of possibilities, but didn't find any completely convincing. Of course, I had done the opposite of what I should have done: a surprise wouldn't be a surprise if it didn't have the surprise factor! In the end, I succumbed to waiting and trusting.

And lo and behold, over the last few chapters, a shift took place. I realised more and more that Reiki wasn't just a complementary therapy, but a lifestyle. This was accompanied by an even bigger shift. I had always seen Reiki as a *personal* lifestyle – a tool for personal development, a way of making an individual spiritual connection and accessing personal guidance and healing. Then it came to me: in effect, that was saying, 'The rest of the world may be struggling, but *I'm* on the right path. I'm alright, Jack!'

And that was a huge mistake. Because we *are* the world. The world is as it is because of us. It is an outer representation of our own inner world.

I know this is hard to take in. And feels pretty unfair. I mean, just look at the state of the planet: war and famine, injustice and inequality, theft, rape and murder, accidents, illnesses, exploitation, pollution; continent standing against continent, country against country, religion against religion, majority against minority (and sometimes the other way around), gender against gender, skin colour against skin colour, ethnicity against ethnicity... Furthermore, we have reached a point in human history where we cannot just harm one another, but the entire planet. We are technologically so advanced that we can make the entire population extinct and even blow up the planet if we wish.

And all this is on the daily news, and in our daily lives, until eventually we can't bear it anymore. Our self-preservation instinct kicks in and we realise we need to switch off and have a nice dinner, watch a relaxing movie, do some exercise, or go for a walk and look at the trees and the sky and listen to the birds.

Eventually, the switching-off becomes the norm and we decide not to let all the negativity in the world get to us anymore.

But there's no escape. Even if we're totally oblivious to the state of the world, we may take our daily walk and suddenly see something we don't like: litter on the path, a broken park bench or a closed coffee shop. It may be something really small, but it triggers something inside us and we start an internal conversation: '*Why* aren't these idiots taking their rubbish home? Or at least putting it in a bin? Why are things *always* broken? Why can I *never* get a coffee when I want one?' Then we remember that yesterday we noticed a fresh scratch on our car. And our partner didn't seem to care. Before long, we are filled with anger.

Then our phone rings and a colleague asks a question. How *dare* they phone us on our day off?! Now we are incandescent with rage.

Just a few tiny problems, none with any lasting effect, and we still explode. It's not the same for everyone, of course – some get angry more quickly than others, some manage to mask their anger to such a degree that they hardly ever appear angry. But we all carry anger inside us. We just have different triggers.

And so does the world. Anger is rooted in fear. And one or the other is behind all the problems in the world.

Internally, we are experiencing the same struggles that are dominating the outer world. The world is nothing but a reflection of our inner battles, our state of mind and our awareness. So there's just no way to say, 'I'm on my own personal path. And that's that.' We're all on our own personal journeys, but we're all in the world – a world was designed for us to experience and enjoy, and to learn and grow and realise that we are spiritual beings and live as such. And we have turned it into a nightmare.

Just imagine that at some stage during our inner angry dialogue, we feel our hands getting warm and realise that Reiki has switched itself on because we need it.

Just imagine we are suddenly reminded that we are connected to a reality beyond these personal struggles. Wouldn't that take that internal dialogue in a different direction?

Just imagine that at any moment the energy in our palms could remind us that we are spiritual beings. That we are loved and safe. And that everyone else is too. Including the neighbour who starts hoovering every Sunday at 7 a.m., our nightmare mother-in-law, the dangerous driver who narrowly missed us the other day, the petty thief who took our mobile phone and the mass murderer who tortures his victims before killing them. They all have their own struggles, with love or fear taking over to varying degrees, but they are all spiritual beings connected to Source.

How do we deal with this? Do we treat them as spiritual beings? That doesn't mean that we should accept bad behaviour and shouldn't take steps to safeguard society in some cases. But we can do this while still realising that with more support and love, the 'difficult' person perhaps wouldn't be where they are now. And they still have the potential to change.

The world is clearly at a tipping-point and karma has somehow brought us all to incarnate at this time. I am sure there is a reason for it: we are meant to make a difference.

That was my big surprise: a political ending to the book. How odd that I had a degree in political science but had never really realised that politics wasn't about party politics or politicians, but about society. About the society of souls.

About living from the heart and building our society from the heart.

Suddenly I began to understand what Mikao Usui meant by 'bringing Reiki into the 21st century'. He meant *using it on a global scale.*

It became clear why, during that fateful encounter in the spa in Japan, he told me, again and again, to bring Reiki into the cities. That is where most people live. Only a lucky and privileged few find work outside the major centres nowadays, and this trend seems set to continue. Cities are growing and growing, while villages are becoming deserted. Usui was simply stating the obvious: city living is the future – but at the same time it is the unhealthiest and most inhumane way of living. Many city folk don't even know the names of their next-door neighbours! And of course, city living is also a major source of inequality.

Reiki can revolutionise every aspect of our lives: the way we think, we feel and we act, both individually and as a society. Just imagine a city where everyone uses Reiki…

But before this final chapter, I did have a moment of doubt: was this really what I was meant to write? Was it good enough? Clear enough? Complete enough?

Then Mikao Usui appeared again and said, with a cheeky smile, 'You wanted to publish this book a long time ago, with only half the content. It wasn't ready and instead you were given the opportunity to write an introduction to Reiki. Now you are writing about a deeper understanding of Reiki and the philosophy behind it. And finally you will write a workbook to implement all this. Do you see now how the timing has been perfect? You must trust more.'

Trust more? Maybe he had a point. I certainly hadn't planned on following up this book with another one. At least not yet. But it makes sense. Realisation is the first step. Application is the tricky part. And we will need all the help we can get – ideas, techniques, encouragement – because the changes needed are radical. What we need is an inner revolution to overcome the millennia-old misguided beliefs we hold about ourselves. Therefore, I already know my next book will be called *The Reiki Revolution* and will present a new movement implementing Reiki in the world.

It seems to me that Reiki can be used either as a complementary therapy or as a way of understanding our connection to the Source of the universe.

That Source isn't in a distant place, but right here, right now. Eternity isn't in the distant future, but right here, right now. And Reiki, really, is *proof of eternity* – right here in our hands.

Epilogue

Karmic Relations

Writing this book has been an interesting experience, and sometimes a mortifying one. It developed a dynamic that often took me in directions that were very different from what I had originally planned.

The first challenge was that I wanted to be absolutely honest, but writing about the difficult times meant that I ended up emotionally reliving them.

Then, when I began to write about my experiences in Japan and decided to include more information about Mikao Usui, he suddenly stepped in himself. As I mentioned earlier, at times I could feel him looking over my shoulder, often dictating or correcting what I had written. At other times, when I was in more of a natural flow, he would stay in the background. But I would often feel uncertain, look up and ask if what I had written was okay. Reassuringly, he would always reply, 'We will stop you if something isn't correct.'

Through all the experiences related here, it has become crystal clear to me that life doesn't end with death, and that we plan, at least to a certain degree, the lessons we want (or need) to learn and the experiences we want to have in our lives.

So it follows on that energetic connections aren't just formed during one lifetime, but several. There may be something like a group of souls incarnating together again and again, playing different roles and allowing one another to have different experiences. And sometimes having the opportunity to transform negativity from past incarnations or to further progress already made.

Mikao Usui told me that his ability to create the system of Reiki was rooted in many incarnations working in Eastern spiritual and healing traditions. Our connection was, as a psychic friend of mine intuited, very much that of student and master, with me obviously being the student. It was a relationship built over several incarnations and hundreds of years.

I had always, wondered, though, how Mum fit into this karmic web. After all, it will have become pretty obvious how close we are in this lifetime.

The online channelling that I quoted earlier already pointed in a karmic direction. I will repeat the relevant section here:

> *You have a mother who is very close to your heart. You are both very connected and very similar in your soul.*
>
> *You have inherited a lot of character traits from her – the ambition, the slight obsessiveness, the perseverance and the strength to get things done.*
>
> *You feel a great connection to and love for her…*
>
> *You lived in a far-away land many, many years ago.*

You were a ship-builder...

When you were in a country surrounded by sea and cliffs, you met a woman who asked you to transport goods on your ships – silk, fabrics and the like.

You stood face to face, and for the first time in your life, you felt love for a woman...

That woman is your mother in this life.

A few years ago, a new friend came into my life. Stewart Pearce contacted me on Facebook and told me that psychic friends had suggested we meet.

We met for dinner at a restaurant in central London and had the most interesting conversation. I had rarely come across someone with so much spiritual knowledge. Strangely, though, it was almost too much. I remember being much quieter than usual. I suppose I somehow doubted whether all his stories could possibly be true.

A few weeks later we met again and I assume my reservations hadn't gone unnoticed, as he offered me a reading. He used his own angel cards, paired with intuition, and started to talk about my life and family.

Then suddenly he said, 'I feel there is something deeper going on here. Your connection to Reiki is much older than you think – it started a few hundred years ago.'

I was just thinking, 'That can't be true – Reiki has been around for less than 100 years,' when he added, 'You were connected to similar traditions – Japanese esoteric teachings that later formed the basis of Reiki. You went to Japan as a foreigner, a European trader, and were fascinated by the spiritual teachings there. You went there often and became really accustomed to the culture.'

I think my heart stopped beating as I asked: 'What was I trading in?'

Stewart's answer came straight away: 'Fabrics.'

So, Mum and I met in Japan hundreds of years ago ... and that was the start of the karmic relationship that led me to Reiki. Could it be true? But by that point nothing really surprised me anymore.

I remembered that when I was still in my teens, Mum came home from shopping one day with a kimono. It wasn't the sort of thing you'd usually find in Hamburg's city centre, but she'd passed a tea shop that had it in the window and for some odd reason had felt compelled to buy it. It was the first of several for her, long before they became fashionable in the West. My sister never remembers her being dressed in anything else in the morning, and she wears one to this day.

Of course, I completely understand if people don't take this as proof. Even though it makes a lot of sense to me, confirmation is often very personal. Do we need it? Perhaps not, but it is helpful.

When my psychic connection with Mikao Usui became more regular, I worried more and more about how to reveal it. It felt just too preposterous. When he told me about his rather hedonistic lifestyle in Tokyo before his bankruptcy, I asked him how on Earth I was supposed to include such information in this book. I said I needed proof – a date, or something else that could be independently verified.

The answer came by return: 'Google your birthday in relation to Japanese history.'

You will remember that my birthday is 17th October, and 1710 was the number that kept appearing when I was in Japan. I started my Google search straight away, and there it was: *1710* was the year Emperor Higashiyama died, the emperor who had presided over the most prosperous period in Japan for hundreds of years. It was a time when Japan was entirely closed to foreign influence – except for some Dutch traders on the silk road.

So, was this when Mum and I met? In 1710, when she was a manufacturer of fine silks and I was a Dutch trader? And Mikao Usui was our spiritual teacher?

Our story goes on and on, but when I started writing this book, I had no idea that it would mark the conclusion of a personal chapter. I worked on various aspects of it for quite a while, but it never seemed the right time to finish it. When the covid-19 lockdown arrived, there was nothing else to do but finish it. I sometimes wonder whether subconsciously I had dragged out completing it so that I could spend more time with Mum. Towards the end of lockdown, she moved back to Germany.

Now the book is written. And I am about to move to the USA.

I know that this is the next step on my journey to bring Reiki into the 21st century. But the karmic bond will not end here.

I hope that you, dear reader, also have a person by your side, a partner, relative or friend who is a true soulmate. I have been privileged to have an amazing companion for hundreds of years.

Mum.

Acknowledgements

My deep gratitude to all the wonderful people who have supported me on my path, especially while working on this book:

My mum, Petra Lange, for allowing me to write so freely about our shared experiences.

My sister, Cosima Lange, for being the love and support she is.

Tanja and Christian Bahnsen, for their loving friendship.

Hyakuten Inamoto, the Buddhist monk and Reiki teacher, for spending so much time with me in Kyoto and allowing me to use his fantastic translation of the Usui memorial stone.

Stewart Pearce, for sharing his intuitive insights and mediumship.

Elke Rosenburg, for her support and guidance through Tarot and mediumship.

Lizzie Henry, my amazingly thoughtful, thorough and dedicated copy-editor.

Ryan Lavender, whose incredible variety of skills helped me publish three online video courses. He also designed my websites and composed the music for my Reiki sound recordings. For this book, he not only took the picture, but also designed the beautiful cover.

And my wonderful students, both online and live, who so openly shared their Reiki experiences with me.

Further resources for Reiki training and support:

www.torstenalange.com

and

www.thereikirevolution.com

Made in the USA
Middletown, DE
08 May 2022